Introduction
to
Women's
Gymnastics

Introduction to Women's Gymnastics

BLANCHE JESSEN DRURY

ANDREA BODO SCHMID

California State University, San Francisco

Illustrations by
Patricia L. Thomson
California State University, Fresno

HAWTHORN BOOKS, INC./*Publishers***
NEW YORK

Contents

Preface

The purpose of this book is twofold. First, it is written for the beginning student, to help her develop as a gymnast. It should give her both an understanding of present-day gymnastics and suggestions for general self-development through practice of the sport. Although the book is written primarily for the beginning student, a few of the skills may be considered intermediate.

Second, the book is designed to give the secondary school teacher sufficient material to develop a unit on gymnastics. It also contains sufficient material for a college instructor to plan a typical beginning activity class. It is *not* planned for the intermediate or advanced gymnast, however. They should refer to *Gymnastics for Women,* a complete text including skills and movement sequences on all apparatus through advanced techniques.

For the advanced performer who is interested in competition, or the coach of a gymnastic team, the book *Judging and Coaching Women's Gymnastics* is recommended.

This introductory book is planned to help the beginner achieve some success in women's gymnastics, with the hope that it will lead to continued physical development through participation in this exciting sport.

Blanche Jessen Drury
Andrea Bodo Schmid

A Brief History of Women's Gymnastics

Since 1928, when women first participated in team gymnastics at the Olympic Games in Amsterdam, there has been a tremendous change and development in the sport. At first the women participated in some calisthenics and, using hand apparatus such as dumbbells, even imitated some of the strength activities of men. Although team events were held every Olympic year, it was not until the 1952 Games at Helsinki that individual events were first performed. At that time the Soviet and Hungarian women gymnasts were the winners in *all* the gymnastics events.

Television coverage of the 1960 Olympics, however, brought into the American home the new beauty and grace of modern women gymnasts, and helped to rouse the tremendous interest now found in girls' gymnastics in both schools and clubs. Many educators began to appreciate the new approach to women's gymnastics, which developed grace, poise, and femininity in its performers.

The 1968 Olympic Games held at Mexico City reflected the tremendous growth of interest in women's gymnastics in America. The United States team placed sixth; and in the individual competition Cathy Rigby placed sixteenth in the All-Around competition (all four events) and Linda Metheny placed fourth in the balance beam. Two years later at the World Championships held in Yugoslavia, Cathy Rigby earned for the United States the first Silver Medal with her beam performance. In the 1972 Olympic Games in Munich, the U.S. women's gymnastics team placed fourth.

In the last twelve years, the phenomenal growth of interest in women's gymnastics has led to local, national, and international competitions, with many more participants than ever before. Most secondary schools and colleges now offer courses or units of instruction in gymnastics as part of the physical education program, and many have teams or clubs meeting after school for interscholastic competition. Sports clubs and Y's have developed excellent programs and have also sponsored summer camps and clinics for women's gymnastics.

Most schools and clubs use the material developed in the *Gymnastic Guide* of the Division of Girls' and Women's Sports (DGWS) of the American Association for Health, Physical Education, and Recreation; while other groups follow the rules of either the United States Gymnastic Federation (USGF), the American Athletic Union (AAU), or the International Federation of Gymnastics (FIG). The beginner would do well to start with the routines and compositions of the DGWS and USGF. These gymnastic organizations have sponsored both coaches' and judges' clinics to upgrade the quality of instruction and competition, so that the sport has now become well organized at all levels.

Advantages of Gymnastics for You

Gymnastics has much to offer you as a participant. From the standpoint of fitness, this sport offers perhaps one of the best programs to develop strength, flexibility, balance, and coordination. The skills learned will help you to use your body effectively and gracefully, and will also give you a feeling of well-being. Some of the Miss America participants, for example, have been gymnasts and have shown the effect of this form of exercise in developing a well-proportioned body.

Besides developing you physically, the sport provides a certain psychological elation when you can perform well and compete successfully with others. The gymnastics team or club becomes a very special group, and being able to join it shows evidence of perseverance as well as cooperation. Through gymnastics girls have demonstrated courage and creativity and achieved self-esteem, assurance, discipline, and enjoyment through participation.

Regardless of your individual aspirations — to join a club, to join the school team, or to train for the Olympics — you will find gymnastics an exciting activity and a wonderful way to develop a fit body.

Preparation for Gymnastics

There are certain procedures which you may find of value in your development as a gymnast.

APPEARANCE

Study yourself carefully in your mirror to analyze your figure. How is your posture? Do you have good body alignment? Check your figure by standing with the back to the wall: shoulders, head, and buttocks against the wall, and heels about two inches from it. Try to flatten the low back against the wall by retracting the abdominal muscles (pulling them inward), as shown in the following picture:

For good posture it is important that you learn to keep the low back in correct position by tucking the hips under or performing the pelvic tilt.

How do you look in a leotard? Does it have the right cut for a gymnast? Are your underpants showing? Many leotards are cut for dancers, who wear tights under them. Gymnasts do not wear tights because they are unsafe on the apparatus. You should have a leotard with low leg cut and the underpants should match the color of the leotard. Do you wear a well-fitted brassiere? The bra's straps should not show. Elastic straps are very good and tend to lie in place.

Should you lose weight? A gymnast cannot afford to have excess weight, as every extra pound means that much more energy expended in performance. Strength and endurance are necessary, so a very sensible diet should be followed, with a careful weight check daily. Your diet should include the basic foods necessary for healthful living. Be sure that you have proteins, vegetables, fruits, milk products, and whole grain cereals every day. If you want to lose weight, eliminate fried foods, pastries, macaroni, and carbonated beverages. A good diet, plus the general fitness which gymnastics offers, will help you to realize your goals in body measurements.

Not only must you contour the body, but you must learn to express feeling through body movements, and you must develop a pleasant expression during your routines. Long stringy hair is a hazard in gymnastics; it must be tied back correctly so that it is neat and does not fall into your eyes. The teacher, audience, and judges cannot help but form a quick impression of your general appearance even before you start to perform. They will note your lithe body, well-kept hair, pleasing make-up, and the feminine touch you give to your performance.

CONDITIONING

There are certain facets of conditioning which if understood can assist you in developing the figure for which you are striving. It is necessary to have a body that not only looks well but can be used efficiently and skillfully in performance. Being in condition consists of several elements: flexibility, strength, endurance, balance, and coordination.

1. Flexibility

To be able to stretch with ease takes much work. You must be able to go through a wide range of movement, far beyond the normal positions. To get a good stretch without strain or overtension of the muscles, you must do the stretching exercises *in a long continuous movement — no bouncing up and down*. For instance, if you are sitting with your legs stretched out forward and trying to touch your head to your knees, instead of bouncing forward you should slowly stretch your body downward, going as far as you can, hold for a few seconds, and go down further. This is a much better way to stretch than to go back and forth on each count.

A gymnast must be able to stretch her *legs* easily into a split. To do this, the hamstring muscles on the back of the thighs and the hip flexors on the front of the thighs must be stretched, as usually they are very tight. The following are good exercises to stretch the hamstring muscles, and the hip flexors.

a. Sit with the legs straight in front of you. Bend one knee and place the foot to the rear so that you are in a hurdle sitting position. Now grasp the straight leg and pull the head forward to the knee as shown below.

b. Sit in a hurdle position. Bend the forward knee as shown below. Now take hold of the foot with the same hand and stretch the leg forward and up.

c. Stand with your back to the wall or to a barre. Have a partner stretch your leg upward. Keep the knee straight and rotate the leg laterally stretching it as high as possible as shown below.

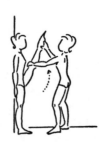

d. Stand facing a barre or stall bars. Grasp the bar at shoulder level. Stand on the left foot, which is turned outward. Hook the right heel onto the bar and with the right leg turned outward slide down the bar, stretching the legs as shown below.

e. In a crouch position or sprint position, place the hands on the floor on either side of the forward bent leg. Try to stretch the back leg backward as far as possible as shown below.

After the above stretches, you should practice doing a split, as shown below. From a split position, practice bending the trunk forward, backward, and sideward.

To perform a backbend with ease as part of a walkover, the SPINE and SHOULDERS must be pliable. Some of the following exercises will develop this skill. They should always be followed by forward bending, to relieve any overstretching. Two good exercises to relieve any overstretching of the back in hyperextension are the Yoga ploughshear and the Yoga rock and roll. From a back lying position, lift both legs upward as in a bicycle position, and slowly lower the legs over the head to the floor. Hold this position for a few seconds, and then gradually uncurl. Then go down to touch the feet in a long sitting.

From a back lying position, lift the head and simultaneously draw the knees to the chest in a tight curl. Hold this position and rock on the back, keeping the back very rounded as shown below.

The gymnast must be careful to maintain a good standing posture with the pelvis in correct alignment, rather than developing a low-back curve or lordosis. That is why the above exercises are good to do after attempting to learn an arch or backbend. However, a good backbend is necessary for certain skills, such as walkovers, and the following exercises will help to develop this bend.

a. From a back lying position, bend the knees, placing the feet close to the buttocks, and place the hands on the floor near the shoulders. Push upward as the arms are straightened and the body forms a bridge as shown below.

b. Stand with your back to a wall or stall bars. Reaching over your head, gradually walk down the bars or the wall with your hands, bending the back in a deep arch as shown below.

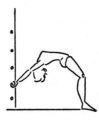

c. A good way to develop the arch is as follows. Take the first position in exercise "a" above. A partner stands in straddle position near your hands. Take hold of your partner's ankles, holding them with your thumbs on the inside of the ankles. Push upward to a bridge. Your partner holds your shoulders and pulls you toward herself. The shoulders should be well over the hands, so that the biggest arch comes from the shoulders and upper back. Keep your elbows straight, heels on the floor, and knees almost straight.

The following movements are suggested to give flexibility and strength to the shoulder area.

a. Sit in a crosslegged position, with arms horizontal and palms upward. Move the arms forward, upward, and backward in large circles Gradually make smaller and faster circles as shown below.

b. Sit in a crosslegged position with hands at neck. Your partner should stand behind you, grasp your elbows, and pull them upward and backward, stretching the arms and chest as shown below.

The *ANKLE* must be stretched too, so that the pointing of the toes becomes a natural part of each movement to give it line and beauty. Freedom to kick the legs high, either in a battement (kick) or an arabesque (scale), takes much stretching and persistent work. The following exercises will develop the feet, ankles, and legs.

a. Stand with the feet in fifth position, right foot forward. Slide the right foot forward, lifting the right heel, and rotate the leg laterally.

Snap it briskly back to fifth position. Repeat the movement several times getting a good lift of the instep and pointing of the toes. Alternate legs. This is called a battement tendu and is shown below.

b. The gymnast should have a very good high kick or battement in all directions. Start in fifth position with the right foot in front. Kick the right leg forward, laterally rotating the leg and pointing the toe, and keep both knees very straight as shown below. This may also be done to the side or to the rear.

c. Sit on the heels in a frog sit. From this position place the hands on the floor in front of the body and lift the hips into the air, taking the weight on the instep and hands as shown below.

In order to use the legs effectively the gymnast must remember to rotate them laterally at the hips so that the line of the leg is better. This should be done in all pointing movements, kicking movements, and held positions.

2. Strength

Though strength is not the ultimate goal of the girl gymnast, a certain amount of strength is necessary to perform the skills. Generally speaking, most girls are very weak in the ARMS and SHOULDERS, and time should be spent daily in building strength in these areas. The pullups and pushups necessary on the uneven parallel bars, plus the use of the arms in vaulting, floor exercise, and balance beam, mean that continuous work is necessary to strengthen the whole shoulder girdle. The various exercises suggested below will build strength in this area.

a. Kneeling, with body inclined forward and weight on knees and hands. Bend the arms, performing a bent-knee pushup as shown below.

b. Front leaning rest position, with weight on feet and hands and arms straight. Bend arms and do a regular pushup as shown below.

c. Using the low parallel bar or a similar bar, extend the body out as shown below. Bend the arms and pull the chest up to the bar.

d. Grasp the high bar of the uneven bars as shown below. From a long hang, try to pull up as far as possible, and hold the position for a few seconds. Your aim is to develop sufficient strength to do several chinups, and even to pull the shoulders up above the bar.

e. Rope climbing is also a very helpful exercise to strengthen the arms and shoulders.

To be able to push off with a strong spring for vaulting, tumbling, or a mount, the gymnast must develop strong *ANKLE* and *LEG* muscles. Correct jumping should be practiced in each warmup period, getting a good push from the heel, through the toes, and on through an extension of the knee, with reverse action on landing. It is most important that the feet and legs be used correctly in any running and landing movements, whether in floor exercise or in vaulting. The knees must always be bent directly over the foot, and not inward or outward. Landing must be accomplished by taking the weight from the ball of the foot through the heel, and bending the knees. Because of the severe jarring of the arches, shoes should be worn in all difficult tumbling and in all vaulting.

Strength is developed by making the muscles work harder than they normally do; hence working with weights or weight training is effective. It is important, however, to know how to use the weights and to know which muscles are to be strengthened. If a Universal Gym is available it can be very helpful for both shoulder and leg work. The following exercises will strengthen the ankle and leg muscles.

a. Pliés or knee bends. They may be done in all five ballet positions.

The five fundamental positions of the feet are pictured below.

First position   Feet turned outward, toes pointed away from each
                  other. Heels about one inch apart.

Second position   Feet turned outward, toes pointed away from each
                  other. Heels separated about one step in distance.

Third position   Feet turned out, toes pointed away from each other.
                    The heel of the forward foot is placed at the instep
                    of the rear foot.

Fourth position   Feet turned out, toes pointed away from each other.
                    The forward foot is placed 10 to 12 inches forward,
                    with the heel of the forward foot in line with the
                    toes of the rear foot.

Fifth position   Feet turned out, toes pointed away from each other.
                    Feet are brought together as closely as possible,
                    with the heel of the forward foot in line with the
                    toes of the rear foot.

An example exercise is the following. Feet in first position, heels together, toes pointed outward. Bend the knees (keeping the heels on the floor), straighten the knees, lift the heels and rise onto the half-toe, lower the heels, and repeat. Similar exercises may be done in the other positions.

b. Pliés with additional movements. Do the same pliés as above, but add small jumps in the different foot positions.

c. Running in place or jogging. This is an excellent way to develop strength in your feet and legs and to build endurance.

d. Skipping rope. Do this for five to ten minutes each morning before breakfast. Skip to music to keep a good rhythm.

In gymnastics there is also need for *HIP FLEXOR* and *ABDOMINAL* strength to perform the different skills. Many moves such as a "V" seat performed on the floor or on the beam are not held positions in a routine; nevertheless, the muscles must be strengthened sufficiently so that such positions can be maintained for a fraction of a second without strain. Pike positions on the uneven bars, as well as kips and many other movements, call for a very strong abdominal wall and strong hip flexors. It is important that these muscles be strengthened, but it is also important that the performer learn to keep the low back in correct position, as mentioned in the section on personal appearance. A poor position of the low back will cause strain, particularly if there are weak abdominal muscles.

Some exercises which will strengthen the hip flexors and abdominal muscles are the following.

a. Back lying, arms at sides or folded on chest. Lift head and shoulder about 2 or 3 inches from the mat, hold, relax to back lying. Repeat (The low back must remain flat; do not arch it.)

b. From back lying, lift both legs 2 or 3 inches from mat, hold, relax to back lying. (Retract abdominals; do not arch low back.)

c. From back lying, lift head and legs and come to "jackknife" position or "V" seat, balancing on buttocks with upper back and legs in the air.

d. Hook lying, arms extended, hands clasped in front of body. Come to an oblique sitting position, passing right shoulder on the outside of the left knee. Relax to back lying. Repeat, passing left shoulder on the outside of right knee while coming to sitting position.

e. Hanging from a bar, back to bar. Raise both knees to chest, extend both legs forward, bend knees again, and return to original position.

f. From a long hanging position, back to bar, immediately lift both legs into a pike position, hold, and return to original position.

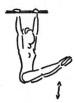

3. Endurance

Gymnastics is a very strenuous activity and makes extreme demands upon the physiological system. Running is about the best method to develop cardiovascular endurance. Increasing the time of gymnastic practice by repeating routines or skills several times will help develop endurance. Half of the routine should be done first, and then repeated with another movement added. This pattern is repeated until the whole routine can be done in good form without stopping. When the entire exercise can be done without too much stress, try repeating it without resting. Top gymnasts are able to repeat complete routines three or four times.

To make the prolonged practice period less fatiguing, background music is very helpful. Either set the exercises to music, or perform the complete composition to music. Music is especially useful as background for practice on the balance beam as it will help you to perform your routine smoothly and without stopping.

4. Balance

Balance is necessary in the performance of every gymnastic movement. An understanding of the center of gravity is necessary in performing many skills. In all support exercises, the center of gravity or balance point must be above the point of support or base of support. For instance, to perform a scale (arabesque), the lifting of the leg to the rear must be compensated for by a forward tilting of the upper body. The performer must "feel" where the center of gravity or balance point is.

An inverted stunt such as a headstand or handstand calls for a feeling of balance in the more difficult upside-down position. The center of gravity must be above the base of support, with hands flat on the floor and shoulder-distance apart. Avoid overarching the back or placing the hands too close together; balancing will then be much more difficult. A good balance position is shown below.

In performing turns, focus or "spotting" will assist in keeping the balance, since moving the head causes dizziness. Look at a spot, and keep looking at it as long as possible, then turn and immediately focus on the same spot again. Try this while doing a châinés turn as explained below. Facing sideways, step to the left with the left foot, cross the right foot over the left, and do a half-turn facing the opposite side. Continue turning in this manner, but be sure to focus on a spot to maintain balance.

To maintain balance on one leg, the buttocks muscles (gluteals) of the supporting leg must be tightened and the upper body lifted, with a feeling of lifting the chest. The muscles between the shoulder blades (scapulae adductors) should be contracted, pulling the shoulders together. At the same time the arms should be relaxed.

5. Coordination

Gymnastics is not the performance of a single skill, or a stringing together of many skills, but rather the organization of a series of movements which flow in a coordinated manner. The development of a sense of timing and sequence is necessary to give a composition fluency and to eliminate a stilted look and abrupt changes.

There should be fluency and coordination within a single movement, too. A frequent weakness of gymnasts is that, although they have learned very difficult skills, they fail to achieve a finished look because of the poor use of arms and hands. Whenever the hands are held in relaxed positions, the fingers should be held similar to ballet hands, i.e., the thumb toward the middle finger and all fingers slightly bent, with a feeling of relaxation in the arms and hands, as shown below.

If the larger muscles between the shoulders, rather than the arm muscles, are used to hold the arms, the shoulders and hands will assume a more relaxed position and will not become as fatigued. Try to synchronize movements of the arms and hands with the complete skill. Do not concentrate on the trunk and legs without considering the line of the arms and hands. This is particularly true for floor exercise and the balance beam. Every day at home, practice in front of the mirror, moving your arms and legs to a variety of music. This will help you to move naturally and with coordination.

It is necessary to learn to contract muscles with the utmost force at a given time and then to release the contraction when necessary. Modern dance training is good to assist the performer in getting the feeling of contracting muscle groups and releasing them. Excessive tension in muscles may lead to muscle strains. Tension also limits the flexibility of the performer and can give the feeling of tightness and "work" to a movement, rather than ease and grace.

It is better to practice two or three moves together than a single movement by itself, unless the movement is extremely difficult. The practice of short sequences of movement accustoms you to the feeling of continuity required for a fluid routine. Coordination has an aesthetic value, as an exercise with correct rhythm will be light, graceful, and alive, and consequently beautiful.

Tumbling

Basic tumbling skills are needed for the gymnast to develop her body and are used in various forms in most of the competitive events. These will be divided into various categories, and examples of each will be given. All tumbling skills should be learned on mats. In practicing a skill, start in good posture and finish in a good posture. A sloppy beginning and finish add nothing to the stunt, and a poor finish gives a poor lasting impression. All learning must be done with the aid of good spotting by a partner, and the performer should learn the spotting techniques along with the execution of each skill. Also it is important to use the complete hand, with palm flat on the floor, and generally to point the fingers in the direction of the movement to be performed. This will eliminate sprained thumbs and fingers.

As soon as each stunt is mastered you should attempt to perform two or more in a series. As soon as you learn a new stunt, add it to the others until you have a sequence. This will help you to learn to go immediately from one movement into the next.

ROLLS

All the rolls must be performed with the body in the shape of a small "bundle," made by tucking the head and rounding the back. Preliminary stretching of the trunk is necessary, and the warmup should include some of the conditioning exercises suggested for the trunk.

Forward Rolls

a. Basic forward roll

One of the basic rolls is a squat, forward roll to stand, as pictured below. To do this movement, squat on the mat, knees between the hands, fingers pointed forward. Tuck the head, chin to chest, and lift the hips, feeling the mat with the shoulders. Roll over and immediately come to a standing position.

b. Straddle forward roll

Stand on the mat in a wide straddle position. Place your hands on the floor between the legs as far to the rear as possible. Tuck the head and roll forward, taking the weight on the shoulders. The legs remain straddled. As you come out of the roll, reach forward with the body from the hips and place the hands close to the crotch to help boost you up to the straddle position again.

c. Combination of forward and straddle roll

As soon as the above two skills are learned, combine them as pictured below, i.e., straddle roll, tucked roll, straddle roll, tucked roll to stand.

Backward Rolls

a. Basic backward roll

The backward rolls call for a good push from the hands in order to clear the head. A ploughshear is a good preliminary stretch, and starting from a long sitting position will help you to eliminate fear. Start sitting on the mat in long sitting. Bend forward, head to the knees, and then roll backward, bringing the knees to the chest as you place your hands at the shoulders, thumbs near the neck. Push with the hands, and roll over, ending in a squat position. To assist you in learning this movement, have your spotter lift your hips, after the legs touch the mat behind you, to help to lift your head through.

b. Squat, backward roll to stand

From a squat position on the mat, roll to the hips and back as you place the hands near the shoulders as before. Keeping the tucked position, roll and come to a standing position. See figure.

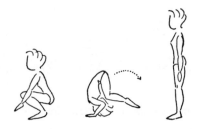

c. Back straddle

Stand in a wide straddle position on the mat. Lean backward in a piked position, pushing your hips to the rear. Place the hands on the floor between the legs momentarily as the weight falls backward, then quickly shift the hands up by the shoulders on the roll, and end in another straddle. Be sure you have mastered the squat backward roll before trying this stunt. Then you will not need a spotter.

d. Combination of backward roll and backward straddle roll

Now combine the backward rolls which you have learned into a sequence. Do a backward roll in a pike position, immediately go into a back straddle roll, and then into a backward roll to squat and stand up. The sequence is pictured below.

INVERTED TUMBLING

Some coaches like to start tumbling by teaching a two-foot limber, in order to get the gymnast used to the feeling of being inverted. Others feel that learning the mule kick is a good preliminary exercise for getting the upside-down feeling. We will start with the mule kick.

a. Mule kick

Standing on the mat, place the hands shoulder-distance apart on the mat and at the same time kick up the right leg, followed by the left leg. As the left leg goes upward the right leg returns to the floor, as shown below. Have your spotter stand to one side and help you by grasping at your waist.

b. Handstand, snap down

Place the hands on the mat, shoulder distance apart and about a foot in front of your feet. Immediately kick one leg upward, followed by the other. Balance briefly in a handstand position, then snap down from the hips as you push off with the hands, coming to a standing position. Have your spotter stand to the side, grasp at your waist, and help you to snap down as shown below.

c. Cartwheel

To do a cartwheel to the left, stand with your side to the mat, kick the left leg upward, and place it forward as the weight is taken on the left hand and then on the right. The arms are straight and shoulder distance apart. Split the legs in the air. Land on the right foot and then the left foot as the body ends facing in the original position as shown below. This should be done in an even 4-count rhythm. Have your spotter stand in back and to the side of you, grasping your waist with crossed hands, left hand crossed over the right. You should learn to do the cartwheel on either side, so reverse the movement to do a righthand cartwheel.

d. Roundoff

Stand on the mat facing forward. Lifting the left leg, place the left foot on the mat, followed by the left arm, as in a cartwheel. As the legs reach the overhead position, hold them for an instant in a handstand and then snap the legs down to the mat with a quarter turn. End facing the direction opposite to that of the starting position. Be sure you have mastered the cartwheel and handstand snap-down before trying this stunt; then you will not need a spotter.

e. Two-foot limber

This is a good skill to learn before attempting walkovers and springs. Stand on the mat. Place the hands on the mat and kick the legs up in a momentary handstand. Then let both legs drop forward to a momentary arch, and pull up to standing as shown below. At the beginning you may use two spotters, who stand with a wrist grasp holding you at the waist and using the free hand to help you up to standing.

f. *Front walkover*

From a standing position place both hands on the floor, shoulder-distance apart and parallel. Kick one leg upward over the head, followed by the other. The legs are split in the air as shown below. Continue the movement until the leading leg touches the floor and then the other foot lands in a front stride position. To stand up again, push forward with the hips and arch out of the movement, the head coming up last and the arms over the head. In landing, be sure to place the whole foot on the floor. When learning, have a spotter stand to one side and place her hand under the low back.

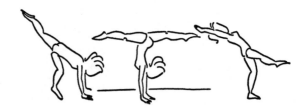

g. *Back walkover*

From a standing position, bend the trunk backward, arms over head until the hands touch the floor. Kick one leg up over the body, followed by the other leg. Legs are split in the inverted position. Land with one leg and then the other. The spotter can assist you by placing one hand under the low back and helping to lift the leg up and over.

h. Combination

Front walkover, cartwheel, cartwheel, roundoff.

THE HURDLE

To perform any running roundoff and running cartwheel, first master the hurdle. The hurdle is a movement which helps to lift the body in order to get greater elevation in all running tumbling and springs. For example, when doing a left cartwheel hop on the right foot (with left leg raised slightly to rear), arch the body, reaching forward, upward, and overhead with arms, and then quickly kick the left foot through to perform the left cartwheel. Try this with three running steps, i.e., right, left, right hop, and left through to cartwheel or roundoff.

When you get the feeling of this hurdle, then practice to have both legs in the air on the hop (left behind the right) and perform a left roundoff as in the picture below.

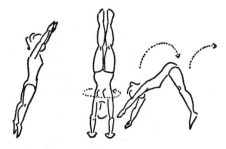

SPRINGS

Before attempting the springs, a two-foot limber and the hurdle should b
mastered. Then you are ready to start the following springs.

a. Headspring from a rolled mat

Place your hands and head on top of the rolled mat, as for a head
stand. Push off with your legs to a piked headstand and let the hip
move forward way over the head; then whip the legs from the hip
up and over the head, landing on your feet in a squat position. Star
with a spotter on either side to assist you lift the shoulders and wais

b. Forward handspring

This should be learned first over a rolled mat or bolster; to soften the
landing the student uses a crash mat. Stand in front of the rolled ma
or bolster. After a few running steps place the hands on the floor i
front of the rolled mat or bolster and spring over it, landing on you
feet. Be sure to keep the arms straight and get a good push from th
shoulders. As soon as you have mastered it over the rolled mat, try t
do it without the mat. Start with two spotters who hold hands in
wrist grasp to assist under the waist and also assist at the shoulder
with the free hand.

c. Back handspring (flip-flop)

Stand on the mat with your back to the mat and your feet slightly apart and parallel. Swing the arms downward, bending the knees as though sitting on a chair. As the body falls off balance backward, vigorously swing the arms upward over the head and then throw the head backward. Push off the mat by straightening the legs. As the hands reach the floor the body is in a momentary handstand, with the arms straight. Quickly snap the legs down to a standing position. When learning this stunt have the spotters use a hand belt or else hand-spot you at the low back with one hand and assist you in turning over with the other.

d. Combinations

As soon as the springs and previous tumbling stunts are learned, they should be put into combinations as suggested below.

First combination: run, hurdle, handspring, headspring, forward roll to stand.

A second combination might be: run, hurdle, roundoff, flip-flop.

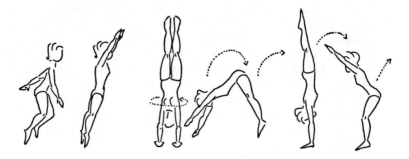

AERIAL SOMERSAULTS

Aerial somersaults are advanced stunts, and should only be attempted after all previous movements have been learned. They must be learned on a mat and must be spotted, either by overhead belt, hand belt, or hand-spotting. Most aerial springs can be learned on the trampoline and transferred to ground tumbling. For these advanced skills see *Gymnastics for Women* by Blanche Drury and Andrea Bodo Schmid, or the other references listed at the end of this book.

TUMBLING PROGRESSION — Self-rating Checklist

Name of stunt	poor	fair	good
Forward roll from squat to squat position			
Forward roll from straddle to straddle position			
Backward roll from squat to squat position			
Backward roll from straddle to straddle position			
Cartwheel to the left — from standing position			
Cartwheel to the right — from standing position			
Kick into a headstand			
Headstand — forward roll			
Handstand			
Bridge — limber. From back lying position			
Standing position, lean back to bridge or backbend			
From standing position — bridge-rise to stand			
Two foot limber or forward limber over			
Cartwheel from a run or hurdle			
Round-off from standing position			
Round-off from a run			
Forward walkover			
Backward walkover			
Headspring			
Forward handspring			
Backward handspring or flip-flop			
Round-off, flip-flop			

Dance for Gymnasts

A good gymnast should master many techniques from dance, particularly ballet skills. Actually, floor exercise and balance beam might be called a choreographed dance in which tumbling and other skills are placed at intervals to enhance and show elegance of performance.

Most dance skills are used to "tie together" other difficult movements, though more advanced dance movements may be used as difficulties in the routine. The study of ballet will give the gymnast the precision of movement, the discipline of the body, and the poise and feeling of projection which is needed by any good performer.

The basic arm positions from ballet which are pictured below are most important to learn. They are best practiced in front of a mirror so as to get the correct position of arm and hand.

First Position
Arms are curved at about waist height. Palms are facing inward.

Second Position

Arms are horizontal to the sides, slightly below shoulder level. Arms are slightly flexed at the elbow. Fingers are relaxed, with the thumb and middle fingers toward each other.

Third Position

One arm is raised in an oval over the head, but in front of the body so that it frames the face. The other arm remains in second position.

Fourth Position

One arm is raised in an oval over the head and the other is curved forward, as in first position.

Fifth Position

Both arms are curved in an oval over the head, but forward of the body so that they are in line of vision. Palms are facing downward.

After learning these positions, try to visualize the correct arm position to use with various steps, turns, and balances, such as a scale or attitude. Experiment to see which line is the best for you, and practice these arm positions so that they flow in and out of the position without any jerkiness. The basic foot positions are illustrated in the chapter on preparation.

LEAPS

Dance jumps or leaps are important elements of floor exercise and balance beam routines. You should incorporate at least two such sequences in your routine. Some of these steps are described below.

a. Ciseaux (hitch kick, scissor kick)

To begin a forward ciseaux, kick the right leg in the air; as the right leg begins downward movement kick the left leg in the air and land on the right foot, with the left foot held in the air in front of the body. This movement may be done starting with the left foot forward, and it may also be done backward.

b. Pas de chat (cat leap)

Stand with the right foot in front, arms in second position. Step forward on the right foot, kick the bent left leg in the air and as the left leg descends, kick the bent right leg in the air. Land on the left foot. There should be a moment of suspension in the air.

c. Tour jeté (jumping turn)

Usually this movement is preceded by a chassé or glissade. Kick the right leg into the air, and quickly change legs as the body is turned to face the opposite direction. It is like a scissor kick with a body turn.

After the twist the left leg will end in a scale or arabesque as in the last picture below.

d. Cabriole

Stand with the right foot in front. Thrust the right leg into the air with the knee straight and toes pointed. Slightly bend the left leg, then thrust the left leg into the air to beat the calf of the right leg. The beat should force the right leg even higher. Land on the left leg with the knee slightly bent. This may be done on the other leg, and also to the rear or to the side.

e. Leap

Spring into the air from one foot and land on the other foot. The leap may be high or low. There may be a series of leaps or they may be done with steps between.

f. Stag leap

Leap upward and while in the air, extend the back leg and bend the forward knee so that the foot is touching the knee of the extended leg. Below is a picture of a stag leap with the right leg extended. You can vary the arm positions.

---

g. Tuck leap

Jump into the air, bringing both knees upward to the head, with head bent forward, and arms backward in hyperextension.

---

h. Backward arch

Jump into the air, both knees bent, feet to the rear, back slightly arched, left arm stretched upward, right arm slightly backward.

DANCE STEPS

To connect the more difficult skills of floor exercise or balance beam, you may use movements such as chassé, glissade, or waltz steps. A few of these steps are described below.

a. Step-hop

This is the same as a regular step-hop. The knee may be lifted high as pictured below, or the leg may be straight in front or to the rear.

b. Chassé or glissade

This is like a typical slide step. The forward foot slides forward, the other foot closes to it, and a forward slide is repeated. Below is a chassé with the left foot forward.

c. Schottische

A schottische step may be done forward or backward and with varying arm positions. The schottische consists of three steps forward and a step-hop.

d. Waltz

A waltz is a step, step, close or step on right, step on left, and close right to left. The steps may be diagonally forward or backward. In gymnastics the waltz step may be performed with a deep plié on count one, and rise to half-toes on counts two and three. It frequently is done without closing the feet on count three to give a flow to the movement.

TURNS

Turns assist in the change of direction, and give variety and finesse to many movements. A few of the dance turns are châinés, pirouettes, battement and arabesque turns.

a. Chainés turns

Châinés turns are turns in which a half turn is made on each step. Start on the right, stepping to the right, turn halfway around. Step on the left and complete the turn. These turns are usually done on half-toes though they may be in plié. If the turns are to be fast, take very small steps to each side.

b. Battement tourney (kick with a turn)

Kick the right leg forward in a high kick. Hold the right leg in the air and twist the body to the left, ending in a scale with the right leg to the rear. This is usually preceded by a chassé or glissade in order to get momentum.

c. Pirouette

The pirouette is a rapid spinning done on tiptoe. A simple pirouette is done by starting in fourth position, right foot in front, with left arm in second and right arm between first and third position. Bend both knees slightly, then rise to the half-toe on the left foot as the right foot is brought into the left ankle, and the left arm assists in turning the body around as both arms are brought in close to the body. The free foot, here the right foot, may be held at the ankle or in a scale or arabesque or attitude.

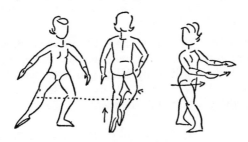

d. *Arabesque turn or attitude turn*

Stand on the right foot, left leg lifted about 45 degrees. The body is slightly arched. Do a turn, keeping the body position. Below is a picture of the same type of turn done with the knee bent in an attitude.

POSES

Many of the modern dance stretches and poses accent movement patterns in a routine. A few of the frequently used poses are described below.

a. *Body wave*

Stand with feet together or one slightly in front of the other. Lift the arms slightly forward and bend the knees and hips. Swing the arms backward and upward as the body executes a waving motion in an arched position by pushing the hips forward.

b. Ballet point

Start in a fourth position with the right foot forward, weight taken on the left foot in the rear in a demi-plié. Slide the right foot forward in a point with the leg laterally rotated so that the little toe is on the floor. Bend the body forward over the right foot. The arms may be in second or fifth position or to the rear.

c. Croisé (attitude croisé devant)

Stand in fifth position with right foot in front. Lift the right leg to a semi-bent position so that the right foot is at about the height of the knee. The arms are in third position with left arm high. There may be a twist of the body to the right, and there may be a rising to the left half-toe (relevé).

d. Arabasque (scale)

Start in first or fifth position. Keeping the weight on the right foot, lift the left leg to the rear as high as possible, bending the trunk forward. The leg may be brought up in various ways, and the arms may vary.

e. Attitude

Stand in fifth position, right foot forward. With the knee laterally rotated, lift the right foot so that the right toes touch the side of the left knee. Keeping the knee high, continue the movement around, lifting the right thigh to the rear. The body should remain erect, and the arms may vary. Below the attitude is performed with the arms in the fourth position.

COMBINATIONS

Dance movements are very important to the total composition in both floor exercise and balance beam. Consequently you should spend considerable time improving your dance skills. Practicing the following combinations will assist you in fluid use of these skills.

a. Step hop, arabesque turn, run, leap

b. Run, stag leap, glissade, tour jeté, scale

*Change of direction

DANCE PROGRESSION — Self-rating Checklist

Dance movement	poor	fair	good
Leaps			
Ciseaux (hitch kick, scissor kick)			
Pas de chat (cat leap)			
Tour jeté (jumping turn)			
Cabriole			
Leap			
Stag leap			
Tuck leap			
Backward arch			
Steps			
Step-hop			
Chassé or glissade			
Schottische			
Waltz			
Turns			
Châinés turns			
Battement tourney (kick with a turn)			
Pirouette			
Arabesque turn			
Attitude turn			
Poses			
Body wave			
Ballet point			
Croisé			
Arabesque			
Attitude			

Floor Exercise

Floor exercise is similar to a dance in that the choreographed exercise includes dance steps, tumbling, and other movements combined in an interesting pattern on the floor. The space within which the performer must remain is 39⅓ square feet (12 x 12 meters). The design of the exercise should include all of the space and should have a pleasing though not too intricate a pattern. The length of the floor exercise is one to one and a half minutes. The timing starts with the first movement of the gymnast and ends with the final pose.

COMPETITIVE ROUTINES

There are both compulsory and optional compositions in competitive floor exercise. Most schools use the DGWS-USGF compulsory routines, though a teacher may make up a special routine for class practice. Optional compositions are also included in competition and this allows the gymnast the opportunity to be creative and to use her skills to the best advantage.

Skills are classified as of beginning, medium, and superior difficulty. These skills are classified in the FIG book of rules. See the last chapter of this book for further information.

It is in floor exercise that the beauty and grace of the gymnast are really noticed. Rhythm, suppleness of movement, elegance of pose, and beauty of composition make floor exercise a favorite both for performer and audience. A variety of slow lyrical, fast tumbling, and controlled movements is what makes the composition dynamic and pleasant to observe. The gymnast should think of it as a dance and should be very

conscious of how she looks to the audience and to the judges. The co
position should start with a dance movement and go right into an in
esting series of tumbling movements. The middle of the composit
should not drag, but should contain a variety of fast and slow moveme
the dynamic and lyrical qualities being interspersed. The.finish should
as spectacular as the gymnast can make it, and should end in comp
control in the final pose. Remember, the last impression is very import.

One of the things the gymnast should remember is that skills must
tied together in an interesting manner by using dance and other st
Hence, in practicing it is important to learn how to get both into and
of the skill. The "before" and "after" moments are almost as import
as the difficult movement itself. It is better to do some simpler skills v
elegance than to select difficult skills and labor through them.

MUSIC

Floor exercise is performed to the music of a single instrument. The se
tion of the correct music is very important, as the musical score sho
suit the movements. Ideally the music should be written for the mo
ment, and this is done in national and international competition. Ho
ever, for the average gymnast this is impossible, so she must select mu
with care. If classical music is used, it should be appropriate. If parts
two or more pieces are used, they must be combined tastefully. To
there are some good records available for practice, and they are listed
the last chapter.

Inasmuch as the timing of the composition starts and finishes with
movement of the gymnast, the music must be carefully planned. A sh
introduction is desirable; too long a passage is poor. The music sho
culminate with the movement and crescendos and accents should fit
action. The gymnast should learn to work with a clock, as she will
penalized if the composition is shorter or longer than the time limit.

TUMBLING SKILLS

Many tumbling skills are used in floor exercise. These should be learn
on mats. The tumbling skills selected for demonstration should be
various kinds: i.e., rolls on the floor, inverted skills, and aerial skills. Re
to the chapter on tumbling.

DANCE SKILLS

As mentioned before, many dance movements are used in floor exerci
These are covered separately in the chapter on dance.

FLOOR EXERCISE SKILLS

There is a group of skills that are peculiar to gymnastics, and many of the
are used in floor exercise. Some of these are described on the next page.

a. Knee scale

Kneeling on the right knee, left hand on the floor. Stretch the left foot backward and rotate the leg outward. Stretch the leg as high as possible, and extend the right arm forward as pictured.

b. Seat turn

Starting in a hook sitting position, swing around on the buttocks, making a complete turn, end facing original position.

c. Balance or "V" seat

From a long sitting position, lift the legs and balance on the seat in a "V" or pike position. The arms may be to the sides, to the rear, or grasping the ankles.

d. Kneeling turn to spiral up

Kneeling on the right knee. Bring the left knee across in front of the right knee, placing the weight on it as you turn to the right; step again on the right knee, step on the left foot, then on the right foot as the turn is continued to the right in a spiral movement.

e. Split

Standing in front stride, right leg extended forward. Slide forward until both legs are fully extended. The arm positions may vary, and the trunk may be arched backward or bent over the forward leg.

f. Split turn

Split on the floor, left foot forward. Swing the right leg straight forward in an inverted split and simultaneously lie on the back. Swing the legs apart in a wide spread, then swing left leg to an inverted split (left foot near the head). Meanwhile turn halfway around or completely around to the left. Continue tucking the right leg to the side under the left leg and come to kneeling position, and continue with another movement.

g. Straddle lean

Sitting with the legs extended and widely spread. With the arms horizontal or holding onto the ankles, bend the trunk forward, chin to the floor.

h. Swedish fall (forward drop)

From a standing position, fall forward, landing on the hands, which are placed in line with the shoulders. The arms are straight and then bend as the head is brought to the floor. Lift one leg as the fall is executed.

i. Valdez

Long sitting, right leg extended, left knee bent with left foot close to the buttocks. Right hand on the floor near buttocks, left arm horizontally forward. With a vigorous push of the left foot and simultaneous swinging of the left arm from the shoulder in an upward and backward movement, push upward and over into a back handstand.

j. Allusion

Standing on the left foot, arms horizontal, right leg in forward point. Step onto the right foot, kick left leg forward in a high battement, simultaneously swinging arms overhead. With a forceful downward swing of the left foot, twist the body to the left. The head comes down near the right knee as the left leg is kicked high to the rear in a needle scale. Do a half-turn on the right foot as the left leg continues in the air. Twist the body to the left and end facing the left foot which comes to a forward battement position. Continue to a split with the left leg forward, or to a front walkover.

k. Butterfly

This is similar to a tour jeté done in a horizontal position. It is begu
standing in wide stride with weight on the right foot, body be
slightly forward, arms to side. Bend low to the right, bending the rig
knee. As the recoil is made, swing the arms up and over and twi
violently to the left. Straighten the left leg and push hard with it
the right leg is kicked out and up. Follow through with the bod
flinging it in a low twist to the left as the left foot follows the righ
Land on the right foot, the head near the right ankle. Continue th
slanting whirl by whipping around to the left to the original positio

LEARNING THE COMPOSITION

One problem most beginners have is to learn and remember the con
plete composition. The best way to remember a composition is to repe
the whole routine several times from start to finish. If the performer h
the habit of going to a point and stopping at a particular skill, she w
undoubtedly do the same thing in competition. She should learn to co
tinue, regardless of how poor one part may be, so that she will n
develop a mental block. If a series of two or three skills is particula
difficult, the skills may be practiced separately until mastered, but it mu
be remembered that the series is part of a whole. It should be put ba
into context as soon as possible.

Another problem many gymnasts have is that of orientation in spac
They seem to have difficulty knowing what is front, back, right or left, a
this becomes particularly true when performing in a new gymnasium. T
to feel yourself in space, and to visualize the routine as lines drawn
paper or a painting on a canvas. The choreographic design should be
well visualized that new and strange surroundings do not cause confusio
One way to solve this problem is to superimpose the face of a clock
the floor and then practice the composition facing in different directior
By superimposing the face of the clock on the floor exercise space, t
student can orient herself to various directions. Thus, twelve o'clock

always directly forward, and six o'clock is directly backward; three o'clock is directly to the right and nine o'clock is directly to the left, with the other numbers giving an oblique focus.

The illustration below gives a typical floor pattern where the gymnast performs on all sides of the square and diagonals, and the line of direction changes from a straight path to angles and circular pathways.

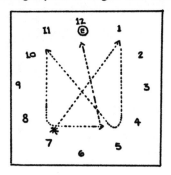

Combinations

Before attempting to make a complete routine, it is best to put together a few of the learned tumbling, dance, and floor exercise skills into a combination. Since the possible combinations are infinite, you should attempt to create your own. These will help you to discover the limitless possibilities of movement. A simple example would be the following combination: châinés, cartwheel, turn, scale, Swedish fall, headstand, forward roll to attitude.

SELF-RATING CHECKLIST

Since floor exercise is a combination of tumbling movements, dance movements, and typical floor exercises, there is no separate checklist for it. Refer to the tumbling and dance checklists.

Balance Beam

APPARATUS

The balance beam is a piece of equipment consisting of a beam 5 meters long (16 feet 4 inches) and 10 cm wide (3.937 inches, although generally considered 4 inches wide), mounted on supports which are 120 cm high (47.24 inches). Any skill which can be performed on the floor is deemed possible on the beam. The skills are classified as: mounts, walks, or movements along the beam; balances or poses either high or low; turns; aerial jumps; rolls; and dismounts.

COMPETITIVE ROUTINE

The length of the competitive exercise is limited to a period from 1 minute 20 seconds to 1 minute 45 seconds and is timed from the first contact of the beam until the dismount. In competition there are a compulsory routine, in which all movements must be performed precisely as written, and an optional routine, which may be choreographed by the performer. As in floor exercise, the skills are rated as simple, medium, or superior difficulty. The beginner usually performs simple movements and a few medium difficulties in her routine. In school competition the DGWS-USGF compulsory routines are used. These routines change every four years. National competition is based on the USGF rules, which in turn are based on the FIG rules.

SAFETY ON THE BEAM

The beginner should become acquainted with the beam by exploring movements on it: she should try walking on it, balancing on it, and springing on and off. Full exploration of the apparatus will help the beginner to overcome the fear of height and of falling. Frequently, the beam is lowered for beginners or when the girl is learning a new and difficult stunt.

At first, two spotters may be used, one on each side of the beam. They offer an extended hand to the performer but *do not touch* the performer. The performer may take a spotter's hand when needed, though if ample time for exploration is given, the usual fears will disappear. However, spotters should be available for the more difficult mounts, movements, and dismounts.

BALANCE BEAM SKILLS

Mounts

Only a few of the various mounts are listed below. The student should learn to do the mount and immediately go into another movement so that there will not be an abrupt stop after mounting the beam.

a. *Crotch seat mount*

Stand facing the beam. Run and jump to a straight arm support and simultaneously lift one straight leg over the beam and sit on the beam, one leg on either side and both legs straight. Change hands to rear support. If you use a beat board, it should be at right angle. A spotter should stand on the opposite side of the beam and grasp the shoulder opposite to the leg which is swung over the beam.

b. *One-knee mount*

The beat board is at right angle to the beam. Jump to a straight arm support and simultaneously bend one knee on the beam, with a hand on either side of the bent knee. The other leg is extended to the rear, and the head is up and back arched. The spotter stands on the opposite side of the beam and spots at the shoulders.

c. Wolf mount

This movement is similar to a squat mount with the exception that one leg is held to the side, parallel to the bar. Jump to a straight arm support to a squat on one foot, the other leg extended to the side. A beat board may be used, and should be at right angle. A spotter should stand on the opposite side and grasp at the shoulders.

d. Straddle mount

Jump with straight arm support, feet to a wide straddle position on the beam, hands between the feet, and arms straight. The head should be up and looking forward. Use the beat board at a right angle and have a spotter on the opposite side grasping the shoulders.

e. Forward roll mount

Stand at the end of the beam. Run and, jumping on the beat board, lift the hips, placing the hands on either side of the beam. Tuck the head and execute a forward roll. A spotter should be on either side of the beam, holding the arm and assisting to lift the hips onto the beam.

f. Step on mount

Place the beat board almost parallel to the beam. Approach from the left oblique angle with left side to the beam. Run and with a one-foot takeoff from the right foot, simultaneously lift the left leg and both arms and land on the beam with the left foot, in either a squat or an upright position. A spotter should stand on the opposite side of the beam and extend hands if you should loose balance.

Walks and Movements Along the Beam

Walks or movements along the beam should be done with assurance and should give the appearance of ease in performance. They are usually followed by turns, held positions, or more difficult movements. See also the chapter on dance, which gives the various connecting steps.

a. Forward walk

Step forward with a definite pointing of the toes on each step. Arms may be in any of various positions, or may move from ballet first

through second to fourth or fifth position. When you are first learning, a spotter may walk alongside the beam offering a hand in case
you loose balance.

b. Backward walk

Extend the foot backward on each step, trying to move with con-
fidence and keep the body erect. The arm positions may vary. The
walk may also be performed on tiptoes. Use a spotter as in the
forward walk.

c. Plié walk

Bend the supporting leg as the opposite leg is swung from the rear
with the knee straight so that the foot swings below the side of the
beam, ending in a forward point. The plié walk backward is just the
reverse. Use a spotter as in other walks.

d. Skip

The skip may be taken with a highly lifted knee, and the position o
the arms may vary. Spotter is alongside the beam as in other walks

Balances

Though classified as held positions, either low as in sitting or kneeling, o
high as in standing or on tip-toe, these positions are held only momen
tarily and should not give the feeling of a pause or stop in the routine
They should provide a sense of aesthetic beauty and a pleasing line from
tips of fingers to the tips of toes.

Low balances

a. Balance seat (also called a "V" seat or pike seat)

Sitting on the beam, hands behind the body, lift both legs from a
bent position to full extension in the air, balancing on the buttock
with the body in good pike position. When you have mastered this
try lifting the straight legs. Later try to balance with the arms lifted
horizontally to the sides. A spotter can stand to one side assisting you
to find the point of balance.

b. Kneeling scale

Facing lengthwise in a kneeling position, lift one knee behind th
other, placing hands in front of the beam, thumbs on top. Lift the rea

leg as high as possible, arching the body. Later, learn to lift the same or the opposite arm, stretching it forward. A spotter should stand to one side, helping you to maintain balance.

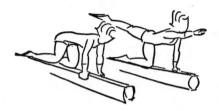

c. One-leg squat

From a standing position facing the length of the beam, bend one knee and slide the other foot forward on the beam, arms forward and horizontal. Later, learn to lift the extended leg in the air as shown in the picture. A spotter should hold your hand when learning the stunt.

d. Lunges

Facing the length of the beam, bend the forward knee and extend the opposite leg to the rear. The extended leg should be laterally rotated, with knee and ankle fully extended. If the lunge is done facing the side of the beam, step with one foot to the side, bending the opposite leg and holding arms in second position. Practice both lunges and try leaning the body in different directions.

High balances

Such high balances as the arabesque, croisé, and attitude are covered in the dance chapter. Others such as the handstand and cartwheel are illustrated below.

a. English hand balance

Facing the length of the beam, bend forward, placing the hands on the beam, with thumbs on top and fingers on the sides. Kick up into a hand-balance position. Practice with two spotters, one holding the elbow, the other standing on something so that she can catch you at the waist or thighs. Practice coming out of the handstand by tucking into a forward roll, or by shifting the body weight forward and dropping legs backward to a crotch seat as illustrated below.

b. Cartwheel

This is the same as a cartwheel on the floor, except that it must be very straight. If performing in the right direction, use the right foot, right hand, left hand, and left foot, all touching in sequence as pictured below. Have a spotter stand on a raised platform or Swedish box controlling the movement at the waist. For details of the cartwheel, see the chapter on tumbling.

Turns

Turns on the beam are difficult to execute because of the small 4-inch area. They should be practiced on the floor on either a chalked or a taped area to develop accuracy. It is most important to maintain a vertical axis of the body, as any tilting forward or backward will throw the performer off balance. Practice the turns listed in the dance chapter as well as those listed below.

a. *Tip-toe turn*

Standing with one foot in front of the other, rise up on the toes and pivot around on the toes facing the opposite direction. To make a half-turn, start with the weight on the right foot, swing the left across the right, and do a half-turn, with weight on both feet. A spotter should stand on either side of the beam with arms outstretched, ready to assist you should you lose balance.

b. *Crouch turn (squat turn)*

Standing with one foot in front of the other and squat down in a deep crouch with back straight. Pivot around on the balls of the feet in a low position, making a half-turn to face in the opposite direction. Spotters should stand on each side of the beam ready to offer assistance.

c. Lunge turn to lunge

From a forward lunge position, rise on the toes and, twisting the body, turn halfway around, facing the opposite direction. Later you might try to make a complete turn in the lunge position. Spotters should stand on either side of the beam ready to offer assistance.

d. Straddle seat turn

Start from a crotch seat position, hands crossed in front (right over left). The weight is taken on the hands, so when the turn is completed you end with a regular overgrip (thumbs on top, finger grasping the sides of the beam) and facing the opposite position.

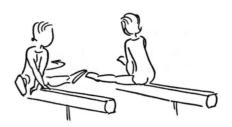

Leaps and Jumps

Like the turns, the aerial movements should be practiced on a marked area on the floor before attempting them on the beam. Leaps, steps, the hitch kick, the tour jeté, and the cat leap are all aerial movements on the beam and should be performed with the same amplitude as in floor exercise. A few other examples are given on the next page.

a. Leap-push-leap

This movement is a coupé with a hop. Leap to the left foot, touching the right behind in a pushing movement as the leap on the left is repeated and the right leg is extended to the rear as shown below.

b. Changement

Begin standing in fifth position, left foot in front, facing the length of the beam. Spring into the air from both feet and change position so that the right foot ends in a front fifth. In the air, the toes are pointed. The arms may vary.

Rolls

Before rolls are attempted on the beam they should be mastered on the floor. You may then attempt to do rolls on top of a horse, or rolled mat, and afterward try them on the beam. A few of the simpler rolls are explained on the next page.

a. Back shoulder roll

From a back lying position on the beam, reach with the hands over the head and grip under the beam, placing the head to one side of the beam. Press the elbows tightly together during the movement. Draw the legs up over the body, and as they are lowered over the head, place one knee on the beam and complete the roll. When the legs are over the body, shift the hands to a position on top of the beam as shown in picture 2 below. When learning, place a pad or folded towel on the beam. A spotter should stand on each side of the beam and assist by lifting the hips and placing the knee on the beam.

b. Forward roll

Standing in a squat position or deep lunge, lift the hips in a pike position, hands on top of the beam. Tuck the head close to the body so that the roll is on the upper back. Quickly change the hands to the undergrip as the weight reaches the shoulders, pulling the elbows close together. Come out of this into a one-leg squat or a "V" seat. A spotter should stand on each side and catch the person at the waist.

c. Backward roll

From a back lying position, reach over the hand and grasp the underside of the beam. In a tucked roll, bend the knees as the legs reach the overhead or inverted position, and push with the hands, which have shifted to the top of the beam. End on a bent knee or go into a knee scale. A spotter should stand on each side of the beam and assist by lifting the hips and placing the knee on the beam.

Dismounts

A dismount is the last movement of the composition. It should be in keeping with the rest of the routine as far as difficulty is concerned. The dismount must also be a controlled movement, with correct landing. Practice landing by jumping off the beam in a straight body position. Land on the balls of the feet first, then push down the heels with the knees slightly bent. A few of the various dismounts are given below.

a. Jumping off the beam

In all the jumps the body weight should be forward and the knees should first bend and then straighten as the position of attention is assumed after landing. Start with an upward jump, facing sideways. Jump off the beam and finish in a good standing position. Now try jumping off the beam with a half-turn in the air, so that you end facing the beam, with your hands touching it. Try jumping off the beam in a straddle position in the air, ending with your back to the beam, as shown below.

b. Front vault

From a front leaning rest position or pushup position, kick one leg upward, then the other, and then swing the legs over to the side of the beam. A spotter should stand on the opposite side, grasping the elbow and shoulder.

c. English hand balance dismount

From a standing position, place the hands parallel on the beam facing the length of the beam. Rise to a handstand and do a front vault off. Use double mats for landing area and have your spotter stand on the opposite side, controlling the supporting arm.

d. Roundoff

Stand at the end of the beam and kick the left leg upward, placing both hands close together in an overgrip across the beam.. As th right leg swings upward followed by the left, hold a momentary hand-stand and come off the beam doing a quarter-turn as the legs snap down to the mat. Push with the hands after the feet have passed the inverted position. End facing the end of the beam. Use double mats for landing and have your spotter grasp the second arm below and above the elbow. In the picture shown below, this is the right arm.

e. Handstand arch over

From a handstand position, continue the arch, bringing the feet over to the mat. Push with the hands after the feet pass the vertical position. Use two spotters, grasping the elbow and shoulder.

MAKING THE COMPOSITION

Before attempting to make a complete routine of 1 minute 20 seconds or longer, it is best to put together a few of the learned skills into a combination. The skills may be selected from compulsory routines such as those of the DGWS-USGF, or the teacher or performer may wish to make up an optional set of movements. There should be a mount, some movement along the beam, some slightly held position, a turn, and a dismount. An example of composition from the skills already presented is as follows.

> Crotch seat mount; swing to "V" seat; swing legs back to squat; walk forward, r, l, r; step left to tip-toe turn; scale; run leap; squat; forward roll to one leg squat; stand up; one-fourth turn; straddle jump off. (As new skills are learned, they may be substituted or the routine may be lengthened.)

*Change of direction

BEAM PROGRESSION — Self-rating Checklist

Note: Start to work simultaneously on a basic mount, basic movements along the beam, a turn, a balance, a leap, and a dismount. You may try all of these skills and then decide which ones fit you and which you would like to put in your routine.

Beam movement	poor	fair	good
Mounts			
Crotch seat			
One-knee			
Wolf mount			
Straddle			
Forward roll			
Step on			
Walks			
Forward walk			
Backward walk			
Plié walk			
Running			
Step-hop			
Skip			
*Chassé			
*Waltz			
Balances			
Balance seat			
Kneeling scale			
One-leg squat			
Lunge			
*Scale			
*Croisé			
*Attitude			
English hand balance			
**Cartwheel			

Beam movement	poor	fair	good
Turns			
Tip-toe			
Crouch			
Lunge turn to lunge			
Straddle seat			
*Battement tourney			
*Pirouette			
*Arabesque			
Leaps and Jumps			
Leap-push-leap			
Changement			
*Leap			
*Cat leap			
*Hitch kick			
*Stag leap			
*Tuck jump			
*Tour jeté			
Rolls			
Back shoulder			
Forward roll			
Backward roll			
Dismounts			
Jump off beam			
Jump off beam with a half turn			
Jump off beam with straddle			
Front vault			
English hand balance			
Roundoff			
Handstand arch over			

* See Dance
**See Tumbling

Uneven Parallel Bars

The uneven parallel bars were introduced in 1938 in Czechoslovakia at the Sokol games and in Prague at the World Championships. They were officially accepted as part of the Olympic Games only in 1952. Since then there has been a tremendous development of the unique skills and thrilling movements performed on this apparatus. Generally, the uneven parallel bars have become the most challenging apparatus to the gymnast because of the uniqueness of the skills performed on it.

The height of the upper or high bar is 2.30 meters (7 feet 6½ inches); the height of the low bar is 1.50 meters (4 feet 11 inches). The height of the bars may not be changed, but the distance between the bars may be adjusted to fit the performer. A minimum distance of 54 cm (21.27 inches) and a maximum of 78 cm (30.28 inches) is allowed between the bars.

COMPETITIVE ROUTINE

There is no time limit on the performance on the uneven parallel bars though usually an exercise consists of 12 to 18 movements and generally takes less than a minute to perform. The movement must be continuous with only two hesitations allowed for preparation for difficult movements. The composition consists of a mount; movements on the low bar, on the high bar, and between bars; and a dismount. The exercises performed on the uneven parallel bars are primarily swinging, kipping, circling, and twisting movements, with releases and regrasps.

SAFETY

The equipment should be checked before each use to see that all supports are tight and in place. Mats should be under the bars, with double thickness for difficult dismounts.

Gymnastic chalk is used on the bars and hands to avoid slipping. Spotters must learn to stand in the most advantageous spot according to the movement. Beginners usually have two spotters: one to help support the arms and shoulders, and the other to give a boost where needed.

If progression is correctly planned, one movement will lead to the next as strength and skill are perfected. Start with the basics and progress as skills are mastered. Do not attempt to do difficult skills until you are ready.

You may experience blisters (which often tear) on the hands when first performing on the uneven parallel bars. The removal of all rings is a must to avoid blisters and unnecessary calluses. It may be wise to use handguards when learning. The bars must be kept clean of chalk by frequent sanding with fine sandpaper to prevent blisters on your palms. You should keep your hands soft with hand lotion. If your hands are sore it is advisable to refrain from practicing on the bar for a day or two.

POSITIONS

The most important positions of the gymnast on the apparatus are shown below.

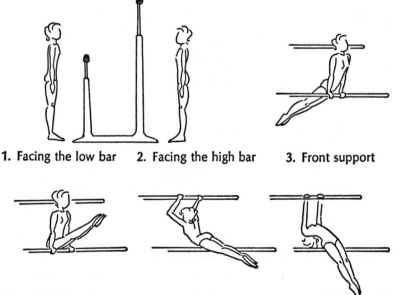

1. Facing the low bar   2. Facing the high bar   3. Front support

4. Rear support   5. Front lying position   6. Rear lying position

GRIPS

The various grips used on the uneven parallel bars are shown below.

a. Regular (overgrip)

With thumbs turned toward each other and grasping the bar on the opposite side from fingers (hand pronated).

b. Reverse (undergrip)

The opposite of the regular grip. Thumbs point in opposite directions (hands supinated).

c. Combined (mixed grip)

One hand is in regular grip, the other in reverse grip.

d. Eagle grip (dislocate grip)

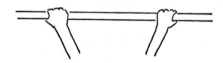

UNEVEN PARALLEL BARS SKILLS

Most of the movements can be learned on the low bar and then transferred to the high bar. Start with two spotters, then gradually use only one spotter. Even Olympic performers depend upon a coach to be ready to assist them on a difficult movement.

Mounts

The mount should be selected according to the ability of the performer. A very difficult mount followed by simple movements is a poor choice. In learning a mount, the performer should go immediately into another movement so that there will not be a pause in the performance. Actually performing 3 or 4 movements together is a better way to practice, because you will then get the feeling of the flow of movement, rather than jerky isolated skills put together.

a. *Straight arm support mount (front support mount)*

Stand facing either the low bar or high bar, arms shoulder-distance apart. Grasp the low bar in a regular grip. Jump into the air and simultaneously push down on the arms, straightening the elbows. End with weight resting on the upper thighs, arms straight, back slightly arched, head up, and toes pointed.

b. *Shoot over low bar (from long hang on high bar)*

Stand behind the high bar facing it. Jump and grasp the high bar with an overgrip. Immediately swing the legs forward under the low bar, then backward. At the end of the back swing the hips are bent sharply and the legs lifted over the low bar, ending with the thighs resting on the low bar. You may vary this mount by performing in a squat, straddle, or pike position.

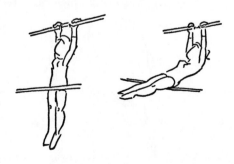

c. Cross seat mount

Stand between the bars facing the length with the right shoulde
toward the low bar. Jump up and grasp the high bar with the le
hand in an over position, and grasp the low bar with the right han
Immediately straighten the right arm and swing the legs up over th
low bar, ending in a cross seat position.

d. Back-hip pullover mount

Stand facing the low bar with hands grasping the low bar in an ove
grip. Pull in toward the bar with the arms and kick one leg from th
hip upward and over the top of the bar, immediately following wi
the other leg. Continue circling until the body finishes in a straig
arm support position on top of the bar.

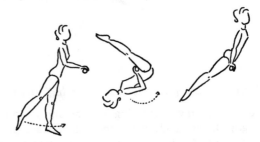

e. Double-leg stemrise mount

Stand in back of the high bar, facing the low bar. Jump and grasp t
high bar and tuck the feet to the low bar. Push with both feet a
rise to a straight arm support on the high bar, facing the low b

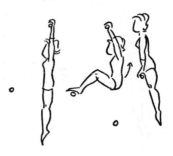

f. Front hip circle mount

Using a Reuther board, face either the low bar or the high bar. Run and take off, arching the body into an almost horizontal swan. The upper thighs should contact the low bar while the body is arched in a swan position, arms extended upward as in the first picture below. Immediately bend the hips, whipping the upper body and arms downward under the low bar. Maintain a good pike position and rotate around the bar. As the body passes under the bar, grasp the bar in a regular grip and pull the upper body to a position directly over the hands as the legs swing to the rear. End in a front support position. Have a spotter stand in front of the low bar and place one hand momentarily on the legs as the body is in the swan arched position. This will control any forward thrust. Then the spotter can assist you to a front support.

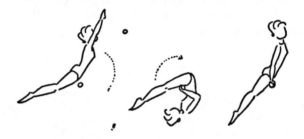

g. Vault mounts (to catch high bar)

Start facing the low bar, and use a beat board. You may do a flank vault, squat vault, stoop vault, or straddle vault mount over the low bar, catching high bar. A flank mount is pictured below. See the chapter on vaulting for description of the other vaults. For a right flank vault, run and place the hands on the low bar. As the legs are lifted from the hips in a straight position up and to the right over the low bar, quickly grasp the high bar with the right hand. End facing the high bar in an inner seat position. Have a spotter in front of the low bar to help you lift the hips if necessary.

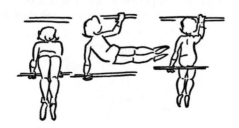

h. Glide kip mount

This may be done from a position facing outward or inward. Stand facing the high bar, hands on the low bar in overgrip. Jump into the air, lifting the hips up and backward, with head in normal position, and glide forward with the feet a few inches off the mat. Upon reaching the full extension position, pike the body sharply and bring the ankles up toward the bar. Continue the gliding action from the ankle up through the leg until the bar is at hip level and head is forward. Then kick outward and downward with the legs, pulling strongly with the arms, and finish in front support.

On the hip lift to the rear, the spotter should stand beside you and push at the hip to get a good pike position (left hand). Then in the gliding position, the spotter should press under the hips to give the feeling of full extension (right hand). At the pike, she should support the low back with one hand and try to push the hips to the bar with the other. On the kick outward and downward, the spotter should assist the leg movement.

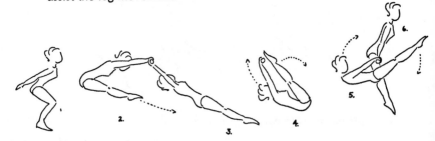

Balance or Held Positions

Some held positions may be used by beginners only to give them the feeling of security and to help them feel success. However, it should be impressed upon them that these are only pauses or preparation for more difficult movements.

a. "V" seat

Extend both legs in the air while sitting on the low bar. As pictured below, the right arm supports in back of the body and the left arm grasps the high bar. Later try to let go with the right hand.

b. One-leg squat

The right foot is on the low bar, with the body in a squat position. The left leg is extended and should be held above the low bar. The right hand is on the low bar in front of the right foot, and the left hand is on the high bar in a regular grip. The position may be reversed.

c. Scale

Standing with the right foot on the low bar and the left hand holding onto the high bar, extend the left leg to the rear and the right arm forward, getting a good arch in the body.

d. Swan balance

This may be performed facing inward or outward and on either bar. From a front support position, find the point of balance on the thighs at the groin. Keep the body arched, the legs extended, and the toes pointed, and lift the arms sideward or upward off the bar.

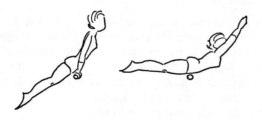

e. Arch through

From a long hang on the high bar, facing the low bar (at the end o
a rearward swing) pike and quickly place the feet on the low bar
Bend the knees and push the head and shoulders forward, arching th
body through the bars. End in a rear stand, changing the hands to a
overgrip.

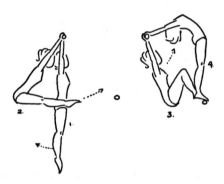

f. Squat stand

From a front support position on the low bar, swing the legs forwar
and then forcefully backward to a free front support position. At th
height of the rear swing bring the knees to the chest and place th
toes on the bar between the hands.

g. Side handstand

From a front support position on the high bar, raise the arms horizon
tally and reach forward, grasping the low bar with a regular grip. Pus
the body off the high bar to a handstand position, holding it momer
tarily and returning to the original position. When you get the feelin
of the handstand, follow it with one of the following movements:
  1. Squat through between the hands.
  2. Stoop through between the hands.

3. Straddle the legs and pass them under the high bar, swinging the
   legs downward to a backward hip circle to a front support on the
   low bar.

Your spotter should stand in front of the low bar to one side and
support the wrist and shoulder during the movement.

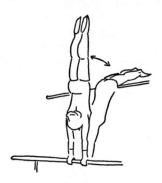

Circling Movements

Circling movements may be done either forward or backward. The axis
is usually at the hip or groin, and the performer must learn to know when
to pike and when trunk extension occurs. Some of the easier circling
movements are as follows.

a. Hip circle backward

Hands in regular grip, thumbs to the rear. Keeping both elbows
straight, lift the weight onto the hands. Swing both legs from the hips
forward and then backward to a free front support. (See cast-
swinging movements.) Whip the legs from the hip forward in a pike
position under the bar. When in the inverted position, pike the body
slightly, keeping the bar in position at the groin. Have a spotter stand
to one side and assist, boosting you at the hips.

b. Single-knee circle backward

Start in a stride support position, hands in a regular grip. Lift the weight off the bar with straight arms. Swing the rear leg backward as the front knee bends around the bar. Drop the trunk to the rear, keeping the head up and the trunk moderately arched. Continue the movement around the bar, ending in the starting position. Have a spotter stand to one side in front of the low bar and reach under the bar with one hand to grasp your wrist with palm facing outward. (The spotter should see back of her own hand.) As you rotate she should assist you (also with her other hand) at the shoulder to help you return to the original position.

c. Hip circle forward

Use regular grip with thumbs to the rear in this movement. From the front support position on the high bar or low bar, lift the weight onto the hands and thighs, arch the body, and, leading with the chest, circle forward in a complete circle. Keep the bar at the hip joint during the circling, and end in a front support position. Use spotting similar to that for the front hip circle mount.

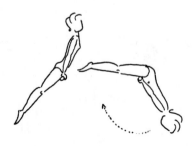

d. Mill circle forward (front stride circle)

From a stride support position, hands in reverse grip, lift the body off the bars with hands, keeping the legs rigid and holding the bar close to the crotch. The trunk is arched, with head back. Lead with the chest and let the bar rest on the rear thigh. Hold the arched position all the way around, keeping the bar close to the crotch. Have a spotter stand to one side in back of the low bar and reach under the bar with one hand grasping your wrist (as in back knee circle), and assist at the hips with the other hand to resume the front stride support position.

e. Mill circle backward (back stride circle)

From a crotch position, lift the body off the bars, taking the weight on the hands, which hold the bar in a regular grip, thumbs to the rear. Lift the straight rear leg slightly and whip it backward and downward under the bar, keeping the crotch close to the bar. Lean the trunk slightly backward and keep the body in a slightly arched position. Turn completely around to the starting position. Spotting is the same as for the single-knee circle backward.

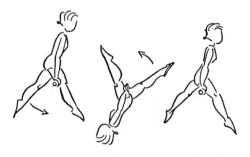

f. Seat circle forward

Sit on the low bar, legs forward, hands on either side of the bar in reverse grip. Take the weight on the hands, keep the knees close to the bar and hips high, and circle the body forward, ending in a sitting position as at the start. The hands must slide around the bar for the movement to take place. Spotting is the same as for the mill circle forward.

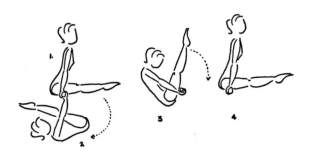

g. Seat circle backward

Sit on the low bar in a rear support position, grasping the bar with thumbs backward. Lift the seat from the bar, taking the weight on the hands. Keeping the body in a rigid pike position, let the body drop backward and completely around the bar, ending in an open sitting position. The arms must remain straight and the bar must be kept close to the seat throughout the movement. Spotting is the same as for the single-knee circle backward.

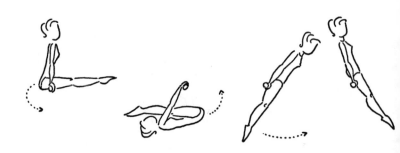

h. Straddle sole circle backward

This movement may start from a straight arm support position or from a straddle standing position on the low bar, hands between feet in a regular grip. From a straddle position, fall backward and circle completely around the bar, ending in the original position. Keep a constant pressure on the bar with the feet, even when upside down. Spotting is the same as for the single-knee circle backward.

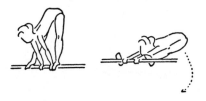

Swinging Movements

Nearly all of the swinging movements may be performed facing inward or outward. The cast is a skill basic to most of the swinging movements and should be mastered as soon as possible. Practice it as described below.

a. Cast

Start from a front support position on the low bar with hands in regular grip. Flex the hips slightly and swing legs forward and under the bar, then extend the legs to the rear upward with shoulders shifted well forward, and lift the body away from the low bar to a free front support position. Then allow the legs to swing back to the bar while keeping the body in a fully extended position. Have a spotter stand to one side and, grasping your arm with the inside hand, help to push the shoulders forward while assisting the lift of the body with the other hand.

b. Cast out from front support on high bar

Start from a front support position on the high bar, facing the low bar. Flex the hips slightly and swing legs forward and under the bar. When learning, you may bend your arms slightly, but later try to keep the arms straight. Then extend the legs to the rear upward and push the body away from the bar until you are completely extended. After the full extension the descent of the body should be smooth as the hips come forward toward the low bar. Spotter should stand behind the bars, placing one hand on the front of the thigh and the outside hand back of the thigh, following the whole movement and giving support to the cast out.

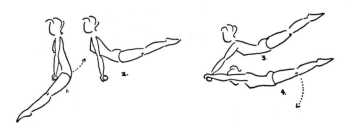

c. Cast hip circle

From a front support position on the high bar, cast out as in the above movement. As the hips come forward and strike the low bar, whip the legs in a pike position around the low bar and instantly let go of the high bar, grasping the low bar. Complete the hip circle backward, ending in a front support position on the low bar. A spotter should stand to one side between the bars, grasping the buttocks with one hand and the back with the other and helping you to whip around the low bar.

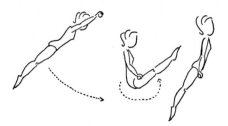

d. Underswing with half-turn from low bar to back hip circle

Sitting on the low bar and facing the high bar, grasp the high bar with a mixed grip, left over right, as pictured below. Swing the legs under the low bar slightly, and then lift them forward and away from the low bar until the body is in a hanging position on the high bar. At the peak of the forward swing, execute a half-turn to the left and, facing the low bar, continue moving the body toward the low bar, contacting the low bar at the groin. Pike, and then release the high bar and quickly grasp the low bar and execute a backward hip circle. Have a spotter stand between the bars. The spotter should grasp your waist and assist in the turn and backswing before the hips touch the low bar.

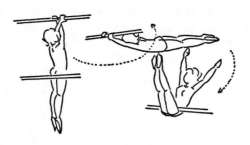

e. Eagle catch

Start from a front support position on the high bar. Cast to the rear and whip the legs forward under low bar in a hip circle without hands. From the low bar the arms are swung up and backward to catch the high bar. Both hands catch the high bar in an eagle catch as you face the low bar. Practice the movement pictured below first by hanging on the low bar and reaching back as you step on the thigh of a spotter. Have two spotters work with you when you do it from a cast free hip circle. One spotter should stand between the bars and step in to grasp your legs as you reach for the high bar. The other spotter should stand in front of the low bar to grasp your waist in case you "open up" too quickly.

Kipping Movements

Kipping movements are based upon the ability to flex or pike at the hip
and then to straighten the body forcibly at a given moment. Timing
most important in learning a kip. A good practice is to learn a tumblin
kip to get the feeling of flexion to quick extension. A few of the kij
performed on the uneven parallel bars are given below.

a. Double-leg stemrise

Grasping the high bar with a regular grip, tuck the feet to the low b.
as shown below. Push with the feet, forcing hips to high bar. Rotal
your grip and push downward with hands on high bar. Finish in
front support position on the high bar, facing the low bar. Practi(
with a spotter standing between the bars to give a boost at the hip

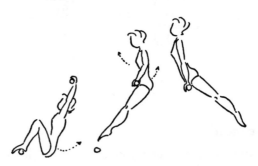

b. Single-leg stemrise (false kip)

From a hanging position on the high bar, swing forward, placing tl
right foot on the low bar. Lift the left leg, toe to the high bar, ar
whip down the left leg while simultaneously pushing with the rig
leg and pulling the body in close to the bar. Pull the body to the rea
up and over the high bar to a front support position. On the wh
down of the straight left leg, be sure to pull the body upward and
the same time push with the support foot. Keep the bar close to tl
body, and let the hands rotate around it. A spotter standing betwee
the bars may give you a boost at the hips.

c. Stationary kip (kip from low bar to high bar)

From a rear lying position on the low bar, as shown below, swing both legs up, ankles close to the high bar, similar to a gliding kip mount. When the legs are up close to the high bar, move them upward and then downward and simultaneously pull with the arms, ending in a front support on the high bar.

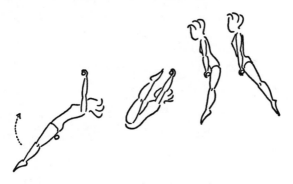

d. Glide kip

From a front support on low bar, lift the hips up and backward (cast) and then glide forward, head in normal position. Upon reaching full extension, pike the body sharply and bring the ankles up toward the bar. Continue the gliding action from the ankle up through the leg until the bar is at the hip level and the head is forward. Then kick outward and downward with the legs, ending in a front support position. Spotting is the same as for the glide kip mount.

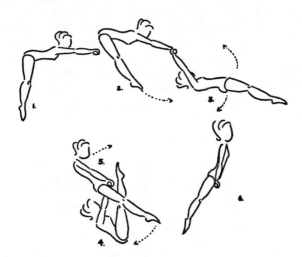

e. *Drop glide kip*

From a long hang on the high bar, swing the legs backward. Then pike forcefully and release high bar. Drop in this pike position to the low bar, grasping the bar with a regular grip. Continue with a glide kip as shown above. Have a spotter stand between the bars and grasp your hips to help you catch the low bar at a right angle.

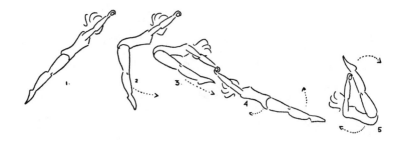

Connecting Movements

In connecting your stunts, it is frequently necessary to change direction: i.e., from facing outward to facing inward and vice versa. Some of the following movements will help you to connect stunts accordingly.

a. *Basket*

Sitting on the low bar and facing the high bar, grasp the high bar with a regular grip. Swing the legs in a pike position through the hands. Touching the right foot to the low bar, bend the right knee and lower your hips while keeping left leg straight over the bar. Let go of the high bar with right hand and, holding on with the left hand, let the body naturally turn to the left, ending in a one-leg squat on the right foot, left leg on the inside and extended. This movement may be reversed to the opposite side. Have a spotter stand between the bars and support your hips as you turn, so as to keep your hips high.

b. Basket with straight legs

The movement is the same as above, but as the legs pike through the hands, continue keeping the legs straight as they slide over the top of the bar, as shown below. Arch the back and kick the right leg up and over the low bar, and simultaneously let go of the high bar with left hand. Continue the movement and end with right leg in the crotch position near the high bar and the right hand on the high bar.

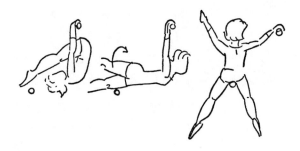

c. Back hip pullover, low to high bar

From a rear lying hang on the high bar, bend one knee, placing the foot on the low bar. Keep the other leg straight. Push with the foot and at the same time kick the straight leg up to the high bar, pulling the body close to the bar. The straight leg should rise up so that the high bar is at the hip. Continue the movement up and over the high bar, ending in a front support position on the high bar. Have a partner stand between the bars and give your hips a boost.

d. Double-leg bounce, low to high bar

Sitting on the low bar facing forward, grasp the high bar with a regular grip. Pulling on the arms, lift the straight legs upward and bounce on the middle of the thighs on the low bar. On the rebound of the legs, pull hard with the arms and continue the movement into a back hip pullover to the high bar. The rebound from the leg bounce and the pulling of the arms must be simultaneous. Have a spotter stand to one side between the bars and assist by giving the hips a boost over the high bar.

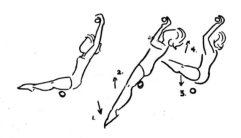

e. Leg scissors on low bar

Start in a rear lying position on the low bar, grasping the high bar with the hands in a mixed grip or regular grip. Kick the left leg up into the air and pass the straight leg over the right leg and low bar, twisting the body as the weight is assumed on the front of the left thigh and the performer faces the high bar. Continue the scissors movement, turning the body to face the end of the bar, grasping it with the left hand.

f. Shoot-through

This may be performed facing either direction and on either bar. From a front suppor position on the low bar, facing forward, lift the body upward, taking the weight on the hands. With a cast, shoot one leg through to a crotch sitting position. On the first attempts, the knee will bend on the shoot-through, but later on, with a greater lifting during the cast, it may be held straight. The weight should be on the shoulders, which are pushed slightly forward on the shoot-through. After learning the crotch position, try to shoot both legs through to a sit on the bar, as shown below. A spotter should stand to one side in front of the bar and support your wrist and arm, and another spotter may stand behind the bar to help the legs through.

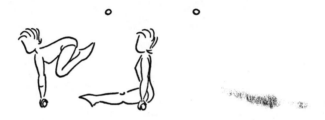

Dismounts

The dismount, like the mount, should be in keeping with the difficulty and quality of the composition. As the performer progresses, the more difficult dismounts should be learned. Some of the easier dismounts are listed below.

a. Single-leg flank quarter-turn dismount

Start from a stride position facing outward on the low bar, with hands in reverse grip. Swing the right leg up and over the low bar as the body is supported momentarily on the left hand. Land on the mat with the left side to the low bar, left hand still on the bar. A spotter may stand in front of the bars, supporting your left wrist and shoulder.

b. Pike position shoot-off dismount

Sitting on the low bar with your back to the high bar, lift the feet into the air and cast the body away from the bar. Push with the hands and land on the feet a few feet away from the bar. A spotter may stand to one side, supporting your wrist and shoulder.

c. Skin the cat from high bar

From a front support position on the high bar, reach down to the low bar with a reverse grip. Slowly slide down the bar until the hips are at the level of the lower bar. In a controlled pike position bring the feet forward and push out with the hands to an arched position to stand with the back to the bar. Have a spotter stand in front of the low bar, grasping the wrist and shoulder.

d. Forward roll off high bar

Standing on the low bar and facing the high bar, grasp the high bar with a regular grip. Lean into the high bar at the groin and roll over the high bar, rotating hands around the bar. Come down to a straight hang position and then, with a small whip of the legs, swing away from the bar letting go with the hands. Have a spotter stand between the bars and grasp your waist as the roll is completed.

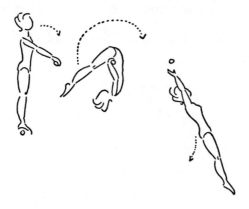

e. Knee circle dismount from low bar (penny drop)

Start in a rear lying position, legs resting on the low bar, body arched, hands grasping high bar in regular grip. Drop the hips downward and bend the knees. Let go of the high bar and swing the arms backward and downward under the low bar, arching the body throughout this phase. At the height of the upward swing, bring the feet under the body for a good landing. Have a spotter stand on the outside of the low bar, placing a hand on the ankles when you release the high bar, to control the knee bending. Then as you swing under the low bar, have the spotter place a hand under your abdomen to lift you upward so that you land on your feet.

f. Underswing dismount from high bar

Stand on the low bar, facing the high bar with hands in a regula grip. Jump into a pike position and swing the legs under and upward under the high bar. Continue the swing to an underswing dismoun Have a spotter stand between the bars and grasp your waist if nec essary. Later try to start it from a front support position facing th low bar, and do the underswing dismount over the low bar.

g. Flank cut dismount

Stand on the low bar with the back to the high bar and hands or high bar in a regular grip. Spring upward, lifting the hips high be tween arms to an "L" position on high bar. Swing the body in the pike position backward under the high bar. As the movement start upward, push downward on the high bar to allow body to rise up ward. Release the left hand and turn the body 90 degrees to the left and then release the right hand and land in upright position (righ side to the bars). Have a spotter stand on the outside of the high ba and move in to help twist the waist.

h. Side handstand quarter-turn

From a front support position on the high bar, bend forward, graspin the low bar with a mixed grip (right hand in an undergrip, left in a

overgrip). Whip the legs out and over the low bar and hold handstand position momentarily. As the body slightly overbalances, do a
quarter-turn by releasing the left hand and shifting the weight over
the straight right arm. Keep the head and body arched during the
descent. Land on the mat with right side to the low bar, with right
hand still on the bar. Have a spotter stand in front of the low bar to
support your right wrist and shoulder.

i. Hecht dismount from low bar

Start from a front support position on the high bar. Cast to the rear
and whip the legs forward in a hip circle without hands. The moment
the hips touch the low bar, bend the hips and release the grip on
the high bar, keeping the body in a piked position until a ¾ hip
circle is performed. Quickly force the arms upward, arching the body
slightly above horizontal so that the straight legs will clear the low
bar. The legs may be together or in a straddle. After the legs have
cleared the bar, bend at the hips and land with the knee slightly bent.
Have a spotter stand on the outside of the low bar to your right side.
The spotter should place her left arm under your abdomen and right
hand under your armpit or chest to help raise the body to clear the
low bar.

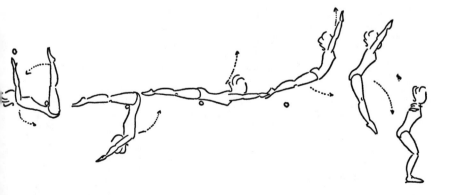

MAKING THE COMPOSITION

Before you attempt to make up a whole routine, it is best to put together the learned skills into a few combinations. When you plan a combination, the direction of movement and body position at the end of a move should determine what the next move should be. Your aim is to create a routine in which one movement flows smoothly to the next without interruption by a stop or extra swing.

An example of a poor combination is as follows:

Double leg bounce off low bar to back pull over high bar, cast (extra swing) to flying hip circle.

An example of a good combination is as follows:

Double leg stem rise to flying hip circle.

Note that here the first movement facilitates the execution of the second movement.

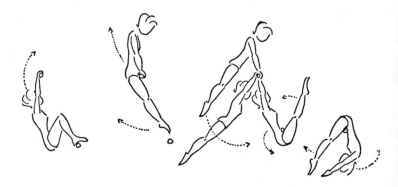

UNEVEN PARALLEL BARS — Self-rating Checklist

...even parallel movement	poor	fair	good	Uneven parallel bar movement	poor	fair	good
...ounts				*Kipping movements*			
...aight arm support				Double-leg stemrise			
...oot over low bar				Single-leg stemrise (false kip)			
...oss seat							
...ck-hip pullover				Stationary kip			
...uble-leg stemrise				Glide kip			
...ont hip circle				Drop glide kip			
...ult mounts							
...de kip							
...lances							
...or held positions				*Connecting movements*			
..." seat				Basket			
...e-leg squat				Basket with straight legs			
...ale				Back hip pullover, low to high bar			
...an balance				Double-leg bounce, low to high bar			
...ch through							
...uat stand				Leg scissors on low bar			
...le handstand				Shoot-through			
...rcling movements							
...p circle backward							
...gle-knee circle backward				*Dismounts*			
...p circle forward				Single-leg flank quarter-turn			
...li circle forward				Pike position shoot-off			
...ll circle backward							
...at circle forward				Skin the cat from high bar			
...at circle backward				Forward roll off high bar			
...addle sole circle backward				Knee circle dismount from low bar			
...vinging movements							
...st				Underswing dismount from high bar			
...st out from front support on high bar				Flank cut dismount			
...st hip circle				Side handstand quarter-turn			
...derswing with half-turn from low bar to back hip circle				Hecht dismount from low bar			
...gle catch							

Vaulting

In the early 1800's the wooden horse was introduced as a means to de
velop the skill of the German knights in mounting and dismounting the
horses. Vaulting over the horse as a sport was first introduced in 182
Men vault from one end of the horse to the other. They also use the hors
with pommels for side horse exercises. At one time women used pomme
but currently women use the horse without pommels, and vault *across* th
horse.

If a horse is not available, a Swedish box may be used for practice,
vaulting may be done over the balance beam.

The measurements of the horse for women's vaulting competition a
160 cm (5 feet 3 inches) in length and 40 cm (15 and $^3/_4$ inches) in widt
The height from mat to the top of the horse is 110 cm (three feet 7 inches
An official Reuther beat board is used in competition.

COMPETITION

As with the other events, there are compulsory and optional vaults pe
formed in competition. Each vault has a point value up to a maximum
10 points. For school and beginning competition, the vaults described
the DGWS booklet are used. For national and international competitio
the FIG point values are used and only 10-point vaults are used.

The competitor is given two chances to perform each vault in bo
compulsory and optional competition. The best of each trial is the offici
vault.

TECHNIQUES OF VAULTING

A vault consists of five main parts: (1) run and takeoff, (2) preflight, (3) arrival on horse, (4) afterflight, and (5) landing.

Run and Takeoff

A good run is most important to develop, and as part of the development of endurance the gymnast should practice running, either in the gymnasium or on the track.

Preliminary practice of running with a takeoff from the beat board and landing on a mat is advisable. Care should be exercised in seeing that the feet, arms, and body are in correct form during running. The focus should be ahead and the takeoff should be with the feet parallel and from the whole foot, with a final pushoff from the toes. The arms swing backward and then forward and upward on the takeoff to assist in lifting the body. Actually the run and takeoff are similar to those used in a long jump. As the gymnast progresses she will want to pace off the distance of the run for the more advanced vaults, just as she will begin to move the beat board away from the horse.

Preflight

This is the time from the takeoff from the beat board until the actual placing of the hands on the horse. Beginners generally use a bent hip ascent, the hips being more or less in a pike position. All the advanced vaults, however, are performed with a straight body ascent. During the preflight it is necessary for the center of gravity to rise and for the body to rotate around it.

To get the feeling of the lift, practice the run and takeoff, placing the hands on top of the horse and lifting the hips upward. Remember that the head must be held upward, with a forward focus. Do not let the chin drop to the chest. The following picture gives the correct position for the bent hip ascent.

Arrival on the Horse

The arms should be straight, fingers pointing forward, and the hand placed flat on the horse. The touch of the hands is quick, and the pushoff should come from the shoulders to bring the body obliquely upward.

Afterflight

From the pushoff, the height of the afterflight should equal that of the preflight, except in the Hecht and Yamashita vaults. The head is always up, with the focus ahead and slightly upward.

Landing

The landing must be correct in that the shock is first taken by the toes and then the heels as the knees bend and the body bends slightly forward for balance. The arms should spread forward, sideward, or diagonally upward, and then come to place at the sides as a position of attention is taken. Practice landing as described in the chapter on tumbling. Use a crash pad for learning vaults.

SAFETY

The vaulter must use gymnastic or tennis shoes for vaulting in order to avoid any adverse jarring to the metatarsal heads at the ball of the foot.

The beginner should have two spotters who will assist in keeping the elbows straight. Later on, one spotter may be sufficient. A secure grasping of the arm is important. This will give the performer the feeling of security and the knowledge that she will be caught in case of error.

BEGINNING PRACTICE

After practicing the run and takeoff previously described, the vaulter should start by landing on the horse and jumping off as shown below.

a. Landing on knees on horse

After a correct takeoff, land on the knees on the horse. The weight is caught by the hands, which are placed on either side of the knees. Stand on the horse and jump down or swing the arms backward and upward and spring from the knees to a standing position on the floor. A spotter should stand on either side and grasp you at the shoulder.

b. Landing in squat on the horse

This is performed almost the same way as the above landing, but you land on the feet, with hands on either side of the feet. Stand and jump off. A spotter should stand at either side, grasping your shoulders.

c. Landing in straddle on the horse

Spring to the horse, legs widely spread, hands between the legs. The head should be up and the focus forward. Push from hands and feet and lift arms over head, landing on both feet. Spot as above.

After practicing the above movements, try to spring over the horse without touching the horse with your feet, as in the beginning vaults with a bent-body ascent shown below.

d. Squat vault (competitive rating 5.0 points)

In the squat vault the feet are brought through in a tucked position, toes pointed. There is a strong pushoff with the hands, and the feet do not touch the horse. Spotters at either side grasp the shoulders.

e. Straddle vault (competitive rating 5.5 points)

In the straddle vault over the horse, the hips must be lifted high and the legs widely spread to clear the horse. Spotters should stand on the far side ready to grasp the shoulders.

t. Flank vault [side vault (competitive rating 5.0 points)]

A flank vault may be performed on either side, but should be practiced on both sides. A flank vault to right, in which the left side goes over the horse, is shown below. Both hands are placed on top of the horse. The hips are lifted sideward, and as the left hip goes over the horse, the right hand is lifted. End with the back to the horse. In this instance the spotter stands on the far side, grasping the left shoulder.

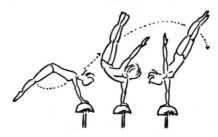

g. Headspring vault (competitive rating 6.0 points)

In this vault the top of the head is placed on the horse. The whipping action of the legs is delayed until the hips are well past the horse. Spotters should stand on either side, grasping your upper arm and supporting your back.

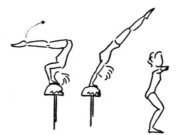

STRAIGHT BODY ASCENT

As soon as possible the performer should start to learn the straight body ascent. This may necessitate a third spotter standing between the beat board and the horse to help the performer get the proper lifting of the body. In the straight body ascent, the beat board must be placed 4 to 5 feet or more from the horse. It is important that the movement be a "flying" through the air, with the legs horizontal or in the lay-out position above the horizontal. The picture below gives the correct body position for the straight body ascent.

The following vaults are the first ones the beginner should attempt to learn with the straight body ascent.

a. Layout squat vault (competition rating 8.5 points)

From a straight body ascent, tuck the knees to the chest while simultaneously pushing with the hands so that the upper body is lifted. As the feet reach toward the mat the arms are extended over the head and the body is arched slightly backward. The arms are brought to the sides on landing. Spotters should stand at either side and grasp your shoulders. A third spotter may stand between the beat board and horse to push upward on your hips. When you have perfected the layout squat vault you may try the layout stoop and layout straddle vault (competition rating 9.0 points). In the stoop the legs are brought through in a pike position while in the layout straddle the legs are swung to the side and straddle over the horse.

b. Handspring vault (competitive rating 10 points)

From a straight body ascent, the arms are held straight and the head is slightly lifted. From the handstand position on the horse the body continues over in an arch, the head remaining between the arms. The body continues the arch as the feet lead toward the mat. The weight rolls from the hand to the fingers, and the fingers and shoulders push as the heels reach slightly past the vertical. A spotter should stand on either side spotting at your wrist and shoulder. A third spotter may stand between the beat board and horse, giving an upward thrust to your hips. Only after mastering a good handspring should you try to do twisting vaults such as the handstand quarter-turn.

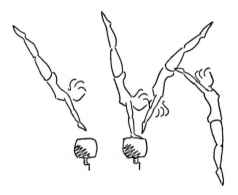

c. Handstand quarter-turn vault (competitive rating 10 points)

This vault is pictured below.

VAULTING PROGRESSION — Self-rating Checklist

Vault	poor	fair	good
Landing on knees on horse			
Landing in squat on horse			
Landing in straddle on horse			
Squat vault			
Straddle vault			
Flank vault			
Headspring vault			
Layout squat vault			
Layout stoop vault			
Layout straddle vault			
Handspring vault			
Handstand quarter-turn vault			

Competition

In the last four chapters we have given the basic information on the fo[u]
areas of gymnastic competition for women: floor exercise, balance bea[m]
uneven parallel bars, and vaulting. These events require related skills, y[e]
each also calls for differences in skill and style of performance. It is impo[r]
tant that the gymnast perform in all four events. Specializing in only on[e]
event is very limiting and should be discouraged. Generally one event [is]
favored over the others, and for this reason more time is spent on [it]
However, this situation should be avoided and the alert coach will se[e]
that each performer tries all events.

One of the most rewarding experiences for the gymnast comes in pa[r]
ticipation in a gymnastic meet. She should compete at a level commens[u]
rate with her skill, and not try to participate in a meet where the gener[al]
skill level is below or above her level. If she is placed correctly with lik[e]
performers, her opportunities for success are greater, and less discourag[e]
ment will be experienced. It is important for the novice to participate [in]
as many meets as possible in order to overcome the feeling of stage frig[ht]
and to understand how a meet is run. She will also learn a lot by assistin[g]
at meets of more advanced gymnasts as a runner, scorer, or card holde[r]
for example. Observing the performance of others gives insight into bo[th]
the combining of skills, and the way others look when doing the sam[e]
skill. Competition also gives the gymnast a purpose for the many hours [of]
practice, whether the meet be within a class situation or between schoo[ls]
or clubs.

COMPETITIVE ETIQUETTE

There are certain rules which the gymnast should follow before and during a meet. The suggestions listed below will help you become a good competitor.

1. Before the meet.
   a. Be at the warmup area at least 30 minutes before the competition.
   b. Acquaint yourself with the lineup and order of events.
   c. Always dress properly. Wear the correct attire and arrange your hair neatly.

2. During the meet:
   a. Acquaint yourself with the apparatus, but your warmup should be short so that others will have a chance to warmup, too. Be thoughtful of other gymnasts.
   b. Keep quiet while others are performing. Nothing is more disturbing than unnecessary conversation.
   c. If you are going to another apparatus, walk inconspicuously at the side of the gymnasium so that you do not disturb the competition.
   d. Never make excuses for your poor performance.
   e. Control your feelings and your temper.
   f. At the conclusion of the meet, congratulate the winners. Remember, treat others as you desire to be treated.
   g. Treat all the judges and assistants at the meet with respect.
   h. Present yourself to the judges, especially the superior judge, before and after each routine.
   i. Do not show by your manner that you disapprove of your score.
   j. Do not complain verbally about your score. Put your complaint in writing and give it to the meet director.

3. At the conclusion of the meet:
   a. Enjoy the competitive experience and compete solely with yourself. Your aim is not to win, but to participate. There is no disgrace in losing if you have tried your very best.
   b. Thank the meet director and all persons responsible for planning the competition. Remember that much time and energy goes into planning a well-run meet, and the participants should show their appreciation.

JUDGING

For details on judging, the gymnast should refer to the chapter on sources of further help. Only a brief resumé of what the judges are looking for in each event is listed below. The FIG Code of Points for Women and more advanced texts on judging will give details of point values for all deductions

a. Floor Exercise

The judges look for the following things: good posture, continuity, movements with proper technique in execution of movements and rhythmical variety. The floor exercise routine must be dynamic and graceful, and the movement must be appropriate to the music. The selection of music should allow for a variety of rhythms with slow and fast passages. The floor space should be used effectively in a pleasing choreographic design.

b. Balance Beam

The routine should be dynamic and performed with grace and elegance. It should contain balance movements including inverted stunts, turns, jumps and leaps, dance steps, and an appropriate mount and dismount. It is better to perform less difficult movements with ease than to stumble through difficult skills.

c. Uneven Parallel Bars

The judges look for continuous movement using both bars while performing swinging, kipping, circling, and twisting movements, with releases and regrasps. The mount and dismount must be in harmony with the rest of the routine. The routine should consist of approximately 8 to 12 movements, of varying rhythms, executed with good technique. No stopping is allowed except for a brief preparation before a difficult skill. Such a stop, however, should not interfere with the rhythm of the routine.

d. Vaulting

There must be a balance between the distance of the preflight and afterflight in good vaulting. The afterflight must be equal to the preflight, except for Hecht and Yamashita vaults. A good run is essential to the development of a good takeoff. The takeoff should be very fast. The arms must be straight upon arrival on the horse, and the weight should be taken with the forepart of the hand in a very short support phase. The head is up, with the focus forward. The pushoff from the horse is from the shoulders and should be sufficient to allow a good afterflight. Landing should be equal on both feet, taking the weight on the toes and then the heels, with bent knees for good control. The lifting of the arms diagonally upward will help control the landing, and the focus will help maintain the position of the body.

Sources for Further Help

Perhaps the primary source of help for you will be the physical education teacher in your school. She will know when and where the local gymnastic meets will be held, and will be a source of help in developing routines. Local newspapers frequently carry news of sports events, and observation at a gymnastic meet will give you insights as to what is expected of participants. Organizations are excellent sources of information, and some of these are listed below.

ORGANIZATIONS

The Division of Girls and Women's Sports of the American Association of Health, Physical Education, and Recreation (DGWS-AAHPER), 1201 16th St. N.W. Washington, D.C., 20036. This group issues the *Gymnastic Guide* every two years and gives rules and routines for school meets.

The American Turners, 1550 Clinton Ave. N., Rochester, New York. This group will give you information on gymnastic practice and competitions in your locality.

The American Sokol Organization, 5611 Cermak Road, Cicero, Illinois, and the National YMCA, 291 Broadway, New York, N.Y. 10007. These will likewise give you information regarding local places where you may participate in gymnastics. These organizations frequently conduct summer gymnastic camps also.

The United States Gymnastic Federation, P.O. Box 4699, Tucson, Arizor
85700, and the Amateur Athletic Union, 231 West 58th St., New York, N.
10019. They both have information on state, regional, national and inte
national competition.

BOOKS

A minimum list of books on women's gymnastics is given. There are mai
more, but a minimum list will help you get started, and each book in tu
will give many more references.

Allison, June. *Advanced Gymnastics for Women*. London: Stanley Paul ar
  Co., Ltd., 1963. Coaching hints for the more advanced performer.

Bowers, Carolyn Osborn, Jacquelyn Uphues Fie, Kitty Kjeldsen, Andrea Boc
  Schmid. *Judging and Coaching Women's Gymnastics*. Palo Alto, Ca
  National Press Books, 1972. The latest book giving a comprehensi
  understanding of judging and preparing for competition in womer
  gymnastics.

Cooper, Phyllis. *Feminine Gymnastics*. Minneapolis: Burgess Publishi
  Co., 1968. Well-analyzed skills and combinations for routines. W
  illustrated.

Drury, Blanche, and Andrea Bodo Schmid. *Gymnastics for Women: Pa
  Alto, Ca.: National Press, 1970. Covers conditioning and dance, a
  hand apparatus, as well as details of basic and advanced skills ar
  routines in all competitive events. Excellent illustrations.

The *FIG Code of Points for Women* is the official international rule book f
  women. It includes drawings for medium and superior difficulties on a
  events and all rules for gymnastics. Order from USGF, P.O. Box 469
  Tucson, Arizona, 85717.

Frederick, A. Bruce. *Women's Gymnastics*. Dubuque, Iowa: William (
  Brown Co., 1966. A competitive approach to the teaching of gyn
  nastics, with good mechanical analysis of skills.

Kjeldsen, Kitty. *Women's Gymnastics*. Boston: Allyn and Bacon, 196
  Good mechanical analysis of beginning gymnastic skills.

Sjursen, Helen Schifano. *Women's Gymnastics S and M Book*. 46 Popl
  Place, Fanwood, N.J.: 1970. A brief explanation of medium and su
  perior difficulties based on the 1968 *FIG Code of Points*.

PERIODICALS

The *Gymnast* magazine is obtainable from P.O. Box 110, Santa Monic
Calif., 90406. This is an outstanding gymnastic publication giving inform
tion on both men's and women's competitive gymnastics. It also includ
training articles. It is published monthly, except bi-monthly June-July ar
August-September.

FILMS

A list of the more recent films may be found in the *DGWS Gymnastic Guide*, mentioned previously under *Organizations*.

The Athletic Institute, 705 Merchandise Mart, Chicago, Ill., 60654, also has films and loop films of current compulsory routines.

RECORDS

Phonograph records for floor exercise may be obtained from the following sources:

Hoctor Dance Records, Inc., Waldwick, N.J., 07463.

Orion Records, Inc., 614 Davis St., Evanston, Ill., 60436.

Kimbo Educational Records, P.O. Box 55, Deal, N.J., 07723.

Index